THE GYPSY AND THE STATE

Recent publications from SAUS

THE GYPSY AND THE STATE

The ethnic cleansing of British society

Derek Hawes and Barbara Perez

First published in Great Britain in 1995 by

SAUS Publications
School for Advanced Urban Studies
University of Bristol
Rodney Lodge
Grange Road
Bristol BS8 4EA

Telephone (0272) 741117
Fax (0272) 737308

Learning Resources.
Centre

British Library Cataloguing in Publication Data
A catalogue record for this book is available from the British Library

SAUS Study 15

ISBN   1 873575 76 9
ISSN   0268-3725

Cover design: Robin Hawes
Cover photograph: The Times Picture Library
Photographic Supplement: Nathalie Beaufils © ATEG

The School for Advanced Urban Studies is a centre for research, post-graduate and continuing education, and consultancy at the University of Bristol. The School's focus is the analysis, development and implementation of policy in the fields of employment, health and social care, housing, social management, and urban change and government. Its aim is to bridge the gaps between theory and practice, between different policy areas, and between academic disciplines. SAUS is committed to the wide dissemination of its findings and in addition to courses and seminars the School has established several publications series: **SAUS Studies, Occasional Papers, Working Papers, Studies in Decentralisation and Quasi-Markets, DRIC Reports and SAUS Guides and Reports**.

SAUS is working to counter discrimination on grounds of gender, race, disability, age and sexuality in all its activities.

Printed in Great Britain by The Alden Press, Oxford, OX2 0EF.

CONTENTS

LIST OF FIGURES AND TABLES

Figures

Tables

POLICY AND PREJUDICE

'Ethnic cleansing', the 1990s' most chilling contribution to the list of euphemisms in which our language cloaks its official violence, is, like 'holocaust', 'apartheid', 'clearances', a comfortable shorthand for the ruthless movements that societies perpetrate against minority groups deemed to pose a threat to the collective well-being. Most of these movements are either decently buried in our past, or are perceived as the excesses of less sophisticated peoples, such as those in the Balkan civil war. But the concept of ethnic cleansing has begun to be utilised to describe, albeit with a degree of hyperbole, the actions and attitudes of contemporary British society to that most maligned of its minorities, the Gypsies.

How valid is such a charge? What is it about the formulation of public policy directed at minority groups that becomes not just protective of the common good, but positively oppressive to those at whom it is aimed? And how does policy develop over time to the point where it can be characterised as offensively as the terms quoted above would imply and yet still be widely and publicly acceptable? It is in an attempt to understand these processes, and their impact upon the people at whom they are aimed, that the following pages are written.

For more than 500 years Gypsies have been treated, for many purposes, as an alien group within the British Isles, and from the first were subject to hostile expressions of public policy. Gypsies are first recorded in the British Isles in the middle of the 15th century and by 1530 there are official enactments recorded against them. Under Henry VIII they were outlawed, and in 1562 Elizabeth I, accusing them of hiding Roman priests, decreed that they should leave the country, under penalty of death. Simply to be a Gypsy, at that time, attracted the possibility of being summarily executed or taken into slavery.

Down the centuries, the endless debates about Gypsy origins, about the differentiation between Romanies and other nomadic people has not, generally, affected the response of the host society. At times this has been hostile and punitive; at other times it has aimed to 'convert' or 're-claim' Gypsies, a process characterised by Acton as "assimilative interference". And, yet again, the response has been essentially an economic one, making the trades associated with nomadism and self-employment difficult and hazardous to maintain (Acton, 1974).

But beneath all these approaches has been the unspoken, consistent presumption that Gypsies should, in the end, conform to a given range of behavioural norms. In short: disappear! It could be argued that policy throughout the ages has posited a form of ideological racism using essentially ethnocentric stereotypes to justify the oppression inherent in action.

In modern times, especially after the Second World War, it was the planning system which, in fact, made the nomadic life hard to sustain and meant that Gypsies existed on the fringes of legality as well as on the edge of social acceptance. Tolerance is the most they have ever achieved and is, for many, all they ask. However, the 1960s and 1970s produced a degree of political consensus in relation to Gypsy issues, allowing a positive framework of law and regulation of sorts, which, for the purposes of this work, is utilised to trace a 25 year history of incremental advance, occasional set-back and periodic concern. This allows us to examine the way in which public policy responds to minority groups of many kinds, and throws light upon the process of policy making.

The interaction between societal pressures and enlightened logic, between the urge towards repression and the spirit of liberalisation, are explicated in the example of Gypsy policy in a way that illuminates a much wider public response to society's minority groups, and reveals layers of ambivalence and contradiction not always apparent in the political life of an advanced democracy. If the end of consensus on these issues coincided with the advent of successive Conservative administrations overwhelmingly dominated by Lady Thatcher, it was in fact after her departure that the first moves to demolish the edifice of 1960s Gypsy policy were made. We trace this process to the present day and describe the confusion and uncertainty which have replaced a clear, if somewhat *laissez faire*, framework for social provision of 25 years standing.

We finally attempt to predict outcomes of changing attitudes in a turbulent environment - of which the travelling Gypsy has faced many during the centuries since Henry VIII devised a 'final solution'. It is not remarkable, therefore, to suggest that Gypsies themselves face these matters with a degree of sanguinity difficult for policy analysts to share. In order to ensure that the book is rooted firmly in the reality of Gypsy experience and is not simply a volume of policy analysis, the authors have, by use of anecdote and of case study, tried to illustrate how high policy at one extreme impacts upon daily family life on roadside encampments and sites at the other.

It is important for the reader to be clear about what are the aims of this book, what its authors have set out to achieve and, even more pertinently, what it is not purporting to do.

In tracing the detailed formulations of public policy as they relate to the provision of services for Gypsies and Travellers, particularly the provision of legal sites, the book attempts to identify those elements which could be said to represent discriminatory or oppressive measures against this minority group.

We understand that concepts of ethnicity, arguments about who is defined as a Gypsy and the very idea of nomadism are complex and sensitive aspects of the politics of difference. However, it has not been our intention to contribute to that debate or to provide an academic treatise which illuminates those ideas.

We have been more concerned to offer insights into the realities of policy making and to provide a link between the inputs and outputs of the political system, and the outcomes as they are perceived by Gypsies and Travellers and those who deliver public services.

Although our emphasis is on the problems of practice and implementation, it has been necessary to give these issues an historical perspective and also to offer the reader some theoretical notions in which to locate what is described, especially with regard to the policy process and to the origins of prejudice and discrimination. In this way we seek to add to the understanding of all those who must make or accept decisions in this area of the public service.

By chance, the issues are given added currency by two recent events: the court of appeal decision in 1994 as to who qualifies under the 1968 Caravan Sites Act to be acknowledged as a Gypsy was closely followed by the passing of the Criminal Justice and Public Order Act 1994, which dismantles the previous legislation under which legal stopping places were provided.

These events are crucial, not only for Gypsies and Travellers, but also for a wide range of professionals, local government policy makers and others who engage, on behalf of the state, with travelling people, and have to implement public policy.

We recognise that these events are also important landmarks in that wider academic analysis of race and difference to which we referred above, and without which the politics of Gypsy issues cannot be fully understood. But it is not the prime purpose of this book to contribute to the analysis of the ways in which 'race' has cultural meaning, central to the perception of relationships between social identity and social structure. However, we recognise its power in shaping the events which are recorded in the following pages and we do not dispute that such debate is central; nor do we wish to avoid the difficulties it represents.

Our rather more limited aim has been to offer a balanced but polemical analysis of the practical issues confronting those who work in this field, to suggest possible future direction of policy and to contribute, however minimally, to the understanding of the way British society caters for the needs and differences of its minority communities.

ACKNOWLEDGEMENTS

The authors wish to express their gratitude to a number of people for their support and assistance in the preparation of this volume; the wide-ranging discussions we had with many friends with a profound understanding of the issues we examine has been a source of great encouragement.

Particular thanks are due to Joan Collins and Mary Waterson, whose vast knowledge of the modern Gypsy story was offered unstintingly, and whose guidance, enthusiasm and practical help were invaluable in the preparation of our manuscript.

We also record thanks to the Gypsies and Travellers of Avon, the Avon Traveller Support Group, ACERT and the Save the Children Fund.

LIST OF ABBREVIATIONS

ACERT	Advisory Committee for the Education of Romany and other Travellers
ATEG	Avon Traveller Education Group
DES	Department of Education and Science
DFE	Department for Education
DoE	Department of the Environment
EU	European Union
HMI	Her Majesty's Inspectorate
MHLG	Ministry of Housing and Local Government
NATT	National Association of Teachers of Travellers
NGEC	National Gypsy Education Council

INTRODUCTION

When, in August 1992, the Department of the Environment (DoE) issued a consultation document on the future direction of policy on the provision of Gypsy sites, it was confirmation of rumour and speculation which had been rife for some months. A new and somewhat draconian change of direction was in prospect. This book traces the subsequent events and attempts to identify the motivations underlying a radical shift of policy, as well as its implications for those directly affected.

The first indication that long-standing policies enshrined in the 1968 Caravan Sites Act were under threat, came from a press release issued by Conservative central office during the general election campaign in March 1992. Issued under the name of Sir George Young, it promised that a new Conservative government would review the Act. It suggested that "far from solving the problem, the 1968 Act may have made it worse by placing an open-ended commitment on local authorities to make provision for those who want to adopt a nomadic way of life". Oddly, the same document had also explained that under that Act, there had been a 30% increase in site provision in the previous ten years and unauthorised camps had reduced by 12%.

The manifesto of the party, issued at the same time, had argued that illegal camping must be tackled, nuisance and distress to householders must be prevented, and the costs to local taxpayers cut down. It suggested that the more recent threat posed by 'New Age Travellers' was linked to these issues. Logic in the two documents was difficult to discern: the nuisance was identified as illegal stopping and the remedy appeared to be the removal of the duty which ensured continuing site provision.

As promised, the new government's August 1992 consultative document (DoE, 1992) made it clear that the review of policy was to be radical. It is not too much to say that it proposed to do away entirely with the cooperative approach to policy on Gypsy and Traveller issues which had existed since 1965. The basis for this fresh approach was that the 1968 Act, which placed a mandatory duty on local government to provide sites, had not worked; therefore it was proposed to remove the duty altogether. The document does not emphasise that under the Act, less than two-thirds of the required sites had been produced. The minister had signally failed to use the powers of direction provided under the 1968 Act, and on several occasions it had been left to the courts to insist that councils and minister fulfil their obligations. The failure was one of political will rather than of policy relevance.

An alternative case

The new proposal suggested not only removing the duty to provide sites, but also to cease the 100% grant for those authorities who wished to do so. Instead, there would be an encouragement to Gypsies either to move to settled housing or to purchase their own sites; there would be revised guidance to planning authorities to facilitate suitable sites for private purchase, but the relaxation of green belt usage which had been open to councils (DoE, circulars 28/77 and 57/78) would be withdrawn.

These proposals were to be accompanied by significantly increased powers to combat illegal stopping. Parking a caravan "for the purposes of residing for any period" on a highway or any unoccupied or common land without consent would become a criminal offence. Even when such camping was with consent, but in breach of planning regulations, the maximum penalty for failing to comply with a stop notice under the Planning and Compensation Act 1991 would be £20,000.

In fact, the 1968 Act had not been totally ineffectual. Under its provisions the number of both public and private sites increased considerably, especially in the decade from 1981 to 1991. The government's original research in 1965 (MHLG, 1967) had estimated that there were some 3,400 Gypsy families, in 4,750 caravans in England and Wales, very few of whom were on legal sites. By 1992 the annual count by local authorities put the number of families at 9,900 housed in 13,500 caravans, 9,000 of which were parked on authorised sites.

So, whilst it is true that only two-thirds of the necessary provision had been made despite a mandatory duty on authorities since 1968, it is also true to say that the increase in Traveller numbers had been significant during this period. This was possibly due to relatively higher birth-rates in the travelling population than in the resident population, to growth in the numbers of Irish Travellers leaving the Republic of Ireland, and to under-counting in the 1960s and 1970s (Hawes, 1987).

The response

The reaction to the consultative document was largely hostile. Gypsies themselves saw it as a direct attack upon their way of life. Local authorities quickly realised that if the duty to provide sites was removed, few would do so voluntarily and the incidence of illegal stopping would inevitably increase. Many groups, including the Country Landowners Association, the National Farmers Union and the National Trust, urged the minister to think again. The suggestion that Gypsies might be 'encouraged' into conventional housing was recognised as likely to produce yet another demand upon an already scarce resource.

At the level of political analysis of social policy, the proposals were characterised by some commentators as an attack upon the civil rights of a minority group and a crude appeal to prejudice and hostility. The consultation paper referred to increasing numbers of Gypsies, to their "privileged position" in relation to planning law, and to the bad behaviour of a few (DoE, 1992). These references were seen by pro-Gypsy commentators as familiar tactics used in the wider attack on minority cultures and were, indeed, an attempt to deny the cultural distinctiveness of travelling people.

The proposals were not, however, without support. Councils which, for years, had failed to find local sites that did not arouse the fierce hostility of local residents, saw in the document a double salvation; not only would the mandatory duty to provide sites be lifted, but there would be strengthened powers to remove unauthorised and temporary encampments.

A number of MPs quickly sensed the electoral popularity in the proposals. On the last occasion the matter had been discussed in parliament in 1990, during a review of the 1968 Act powers, opinions had been freely expressed, but even the most unsympathetic members had pressed for more sites, more direction and greater urgency in completing the programme of site provision. There was less evidence of this from government supporters by 1993.

The private sector option

Another theme of the consultation paper was that travelling people should provide for themselves, should purchase their own land and seek their own planning consents. Effectively this would place what had always been seen as a mainly public provision firmly in a private sector context. As the consultation paper put it:

> People who wish to adopt a nomadic existence should be free to do so, provided they live within the law in the same way as their fellow citizens. This should not however entail a privileged position or entitlement to a greater degree of support from the tax payer than is made available to those who choose a more settled existence. Travellers, like other citizens, should seek to provide their own accommodation seeking planning permission where necessary, like anyone else. (DoE, 1992)

The paper did not, however, speculate upon the ease with which a Gypsy might get planning permission for sites, when under the existing regime even local authorities, with the choice of a number of sites, found consent was frequently refused, and the process of seeking consent almost always accompanied by intense public campaigns of opposition.

On a more positive note, the proposals did include a somewhat muted suggestion that it might be necessary for the government to provide advice on education, health and housing "which encourages Gypsies and other Travellers to settle, and in time, transfer into traditional housing" (DoE, 1992).

It is not unreasonable to interpret that last comment as the nub of the public policy issue: the aim of policy in the long term is clearly to alter the fundamental lifestyle of Gypsies and travelling people in a way which would remove them, as a distinctive culture, altogether from society. A people whose origins, history and culture revolve around the concept of mobility, as the basis for ontological security, would be absorbed into the majority culture in which a house and a relationship to one place are the essential basis for development.

Institutionalising prejudice

This book will trace the passage of the proposals in the consultation paper into legislative enactment and seek to place them within a much longer history of official attempts to deal with the perceived threat to society which Gypsies have apparently presented since their first recorded appearance here over 500 years ago. The argument we explore suggests that public prejudice against minority groups or new cultural phenomena is frequently, in a way hard to discern, enshrined in the instruments of policy so as to ensure that institutional prejudice becomes part of the structure and framework of societal response to those who deviate from the norm. Whether the deviation is skin colour, religious belief or some culturally-based behaviour or activity, public policy can, and often does, legitimise society's reaction, fear or distaste.

The process by which prejudice becomes policy is illustrated starkly in the history of travelling people in the British Isles. However, the lessons have a much wider relevance for the kind of multi-cultural society we are building as we move into the 21st century, in which minority groups of many kinds will feature greater than ever before.

The window of consensus

By way of preface to this discussion, it is necessary to understand in detail the somewhat extraordinary emergence of the consensual, cooperative and liberal period which began in the 1960s and from which the 1968 Act grew. It is an era to which the 1993 proposals have effectively put an end. It was the one interval in 500 years of hostility, in which the concept of civil rights for travelling people was accepted, when serious efforts were made to provide caravan sites, to offer easier access to education for Traveller children and to deliver basic national health services to those without a static domicile or address.

Given the long perspective of Gypsy history in Britain, it is this brief flowering of consensual liberalism which is the aberration, rather than the recent stance of government. The incremental development of policy over this period is traced in detail in Chapter 2.

Definitions

One of the intriguing tactics employed by those demanding a new look at the 1968 legislation, in the lead-up to the radical change of direction announced in the government's consultation paper of August 1992, was the linking of the need for change to the considerable public anger that had been produced by the actions of a quite different group of nomads known widely as 'New Age Travellers'.

These often quite large groups are a phenomenon mainly of the south and west of England, of younger families with no generational history of travelling. The public perception of these groups, often coloured by hostile media presentation of their activities, portrays them as existing often on craft industries, and espousing philosophical ideas originating in 1960s pacifism or 'flower-power'. Their ranks have been increased in the 1990s by many younger homeless people, often as a last resort, for whom the shortage of social housing has left no alternative but to take to the road.

New Age Travellers sometimes congregate in large numbers for musical festivals. They are, in origin, loose groupings of articulate people from the settled population whose origins are considerably different from those of the traditional Gypsy or Irish Traveller. Their vocabulary is essentially one of the rejection of majority acquisitive values and of ecological protectionism.

The widespread anger and public concern, covered sensationally in the press, which New Age Travellers have attracted when they occupy farm land and open spaces for musical gatherings, was harnessed to the support for changes which will mainly, but not exclusively, affect the traditional Gypsy groups. Since the 1968 Act had never attempted to make provision for this more recent kind of Traveller, it is not surprising that some Gypsies feel their case is jeopardised by association with the behaviour, sometimes confrontational, of New Age groups.

Indeed, some Gypsy supporters saw this as the government attempting to capitalise on public outrage at a wide range of relatively new events such as 'acid house' parties and unlicensed 'raves' often associated with a wide range of young people. On this argument, the government's aim was to gain support for more restrictive measures against Gypsies, for whom these activities would be wholly foreign.

But this highlights a problem that has dogged the debate about Gypsy policy for most of recent times. Definition has been at the heart of the argument. Most modern writers on the issue, including Acton (1974), Liegeois (1986) and Clebert (1963), have prefaced their works by attempting to define precisely who is to be included in their discussion; the 1968 Act provides a definition limiting who ~repealed~ is to be encompassed and who is not. For the most part, these contributions tend only to confuse the issues, since any definition has the propensity to exclude or marginalise those not covered. The decision, in 1989, by the Commission for Racial Equality, that Gypsies were a distinct ethnic group, whilst adding legitimacy to the campaign for provision of services, has also tended to create problems of exclusion for others (*Commission for Racial Equality* v *Dutton*). Thus 1993 saw the somewhat unusual spectacle of groups of New Age Travellers seeking court pronouncements that they, too, were 'Gypsies', in order to persuade local councils that they had a right to site provision.

It is for these reasons, and in order to develop the particular argument of this volume, that we need to be clear precisely with which groups we are concerned. First, we use the terms 'Gypsies and other Travellers' to describe the diverse groupings of travelling people of whom Acton lists at least 18 categories, with picturesque descriptions such as Didecois, Pikies, Posh-rats, Tinkers and Rom. They include English and Irish Travellers, Hedge-mumpers, Mumpers and Push-cats (Acton, 1974).

These people have almost certainly never constituted a homogenous group; indeed, as Acton suggests, they are a most disunited and ill-defined people, but they do possess a continuity, rather than a community, of culture (Acton, 1974). The Irish Travellers in particular, whose Celtic origins and background to some extent set them at odds with the rest, are nevertheless so closely identified, interbred and integrated with the Gypsies, over at least 200 years, that their experience is directly related to our purposes.

In this connection, Liegeois, writing from a European-wide perspective, demonstrates that the world's Gypsy populations form a mosaic of small, diverse groups, "a whole, whose component features are linked to one another; a structure that is not rigid but ever-changing" (Liegeois, 1986).

We may identify some of these fixed links: nomadism, or the propensity to live in wheeled and moveable homes, does not mean that all Gypsies are nomads or that all nomads are Gypsies. It fulfils a number of social functions, is part of their identity and makes for adaptability and flexibility as well as social cohesion. For Gypsies nomadism is a state of mind (Liegeois, 1986).

Kinship and extended family groupings are another important element in social structures of Gypsies with considerable intermarriage, a strict sexual morality and a matriarchal culture that delineates male-female roles clearly, through which social control is exercised.

As Liegeois points out, for Gypsies there is no word which defines them as a whole. Their strength is in the very diversity of their life, and their absorption or borrowing from the cultural environment in which they find themselves is achieved without weakening the essential and distinct collective identity. This remains, after centuries of persecution in every corner of Asia and Europe, as strong as it ever was (Liegeois, 1986).

Second, it should be clear that if this attempt at definition excludes some nomads, such as the New Age Travellers, then it will be necessary to discuss the problems which residualisation poses, both for public policy and for those who are excluded.

We argue that although the Caravan Sites Act 1968 and subsequent interpretations by high court judges make clear who is excluded (see Chapter 7), it does not in fact limit the problems of discrimination and prejudice inherent in legal structures. On the contrary, it simply imposes more.

At a number of points in the argument, it will be necessary to acknowledge that those excluded pose just the same moral questions for law makers, and require just the same rights from the welfare state, as those who are 'included'.

It is not, in short, possible to discuss 'Gypsy' issues without acknowledging that large numbers of people who live in caravans do not conform to the generally accepted notions of what is meant by that term.

The New Age Travellers exist on the fringes of the traditional Gypsy communities, on the fringes of legality and on the fringes of our towns and cities. They are, however, absolutely central to the policy issues with which this book is concerned. They will no more disappear from these pages than they will from the landscape.

The aims of the book

The principal purpose, then, of the following pages is to trace through time the response of settled society, as evinced in public statutes, legal action and other policy and action, to the emergence of these Gypsies and other Travellers. For up to 500 years they have maintained a cultural and community identity, and economic and social independence from the majority of the population.

We set modern responses against an historic backdrop, in the hope of illustrating somewhat deeper arguments about the process by which prejudice, fear and antagonism to minority peoples becomes fixed in the formal structures of society.

A detailed examination of post-war policy development on the provision of caravan sites, education and health services for travelling people, is accompanied by chapters which examine these issues at the local authority level and the way such services are perceived by recipients. How have such policies impacted upon the lives of those they were designed to help?

one

GYPSIES AND THE STATE: A BRIEF HISTORICAL REVIEW

Any attempt to understand the interaction between Gypsies and Travellers on the one hand and settled society and the state on the other, must be undertaken against some understanding of the long history of that relationship, its origins and the various phases of official response to the Gypsy phenomenon.

To say that this minority group - and it is still a numerically very small population - have faced banishment, execution, attempts at assimilation, religious conversion, rescue and, briefly, recognition, is not enough. We also need to understand why extreme gestures of prejudice were thought necessary and what motivation lay behind the hostile rejection which has hardly abated over five centuries.

What is different about Gypsies, compared, for example, to the Huguenots, the Jews or other small waves of people who first arrive on British soil? Is it possible to pin down the processes of institutionalised prejudice by reference to the long, uneasy interaction of Gypsies with Britain and its peoples? In this chapter we provide a brief outline of the way the state has reacted to Gypsies since their arrival over 500 years ago.

Gypsies made their first recorded appearance in Britain before 1500, as part of a thousand year long migratory movement, probably originating in northern India. Their journey took them through Persia and Armenia into the Balkans and by the 11th century they were living in the Greek peninsula. As "fortune-tellers and ventriloquists" they are recorded in Hamburg in 1417, in France in 1419 and in Rome itself by 1422 (Liegeois, 1986; Judges, 1965).

Within 30 years of their first documented appearances in England, legal measures began to be taken against Gypsies; repressive laws, some of them with a peculiarly modern ring including expulsion, imprisonment and a ban on immigration, were utilised in a series of Acts starting with Henry VIII's 'Egyptians Act' of 1530. The naming of this Act reflected the generally held belief that these swarthy-skinned newcomers originated in Egypt. The fact that there were four further Acts in the following 65 years suggests that the issue was one of continuing public concern requiring public policy responses of considerable severity. And yet, in contrast to the official reaction, they were not apparently unpopular among the people. Dr Andrew Borde, a scholar who first researched these strangers in 1547, wrote of them: "The attractiveness of these people in the eyes of the wonder-loving country folk was enhanced by the strangeness of their attire and garments. They be light-fingered and use picking yet they be pleasant dancers" (Borde, 1547).

Contemporary accounts tell of them dancing for the villagers in the clothes they habitually wore, dressed "like princes in Egypt" with wonderful head-coverings embroidered in gold. The poet Skelton has them in "rich clothes and rags, surmounted by cloaks worn toga-fashion, hung about them in fantastic medley". It is easy to imagine the drama and excitement they must have created in the isolated communities of rural England. Big parties of men and women, many mounted on one beast, moving along the country tracks, as Dekker describes, with the women wearing rags and "patched filthy mantles uppermost, when the under-garments are handsome and in fashion".

But there is ample evidence that they were feared by the authorities. Savage Acts of parliament were backed by the actions of village constables, magistrates and church-wardens who were not above offering groats and ducats as bribes to those bands who would avoid their parishes.

The 1530 measure imposed a complete ban on the immigration of Gypsies and gave notice to all those already in England to leave at once. In 1551 a somewhat wider Act forbade all "tinkers, peddlers and such-like vagrant persons" to travel from place to place without licence, under penalty of 14 days in jail. Two years later, under Queen Mary, a further Egyptians Act was even more severe; it forbade entry into the country and provided for the capital punishment of "Egyptians" if they remained for more than one month. And at this point emerges the first attempt at assimilation. These penalties could be avoided if those who "prefer the pursuit of an honest calling to banishment or death are willing to abandon the wandering life", they can do so without fear of injury from the state.

(Are there not echoes here of the 1992 consultation paper, with its emphasis on encouragement to settle in permanent housing?)

All of these penalties were repeated and extended in yet another Egyptians Act passed under Queen Elizabeth I in 1562. By 1596 her attack had become a little more subtle. An early Poor Law Act of that year declared as rogues and vagabonds (and therefore excluded from the poor law provisions) "all tinkers wandering abroad, and all such persons, not being felons, wandering and pretending themselves to be Egipcyans or wandering in the habite, forme or attyre of counterfayte Egipcians". This suggests that the wandering Gypsies were attracting indigenous folk to their ranks, or to the itinerant life, in large enough numbers to worry the Tudor law makers.

We may guess at the many social and economic pressures which could have driven previously settled people to take up life on the road in those times, no doubt to add to the numberless peddlers, hawkers, vagrants and beggars which made up the Elizabethan underclass; perhaps copying the carefree style of the 'Egyptians'. With each new piece of legislation, there was less and less attempt to differentiate between the various kinds of itinerant. The 20th century equivalent, in some respects, is the advent of New Age Travellers, who, although of somewhat different background, motivation and culture, become linked inextricably with the Gypsies and the Irish Travellers in the minds of those who contribute to the debate about how 'we' should respond.

It is clear from the frequency and harshness of the legal measures taken at the time that there was considerable official concern about the activities of travelling people and the threat which they appeared to pose to the ordered and highly stratified society of the 16th century. It is especially intriguing to contemplate that the Tudor reigns faced some of the most menacing international threats to the state and deep-seated religious turbulence at home; why, then, was so much attention paid to a few thousand wandering mountebanks and conjurers?

Some flavour of the political motivation of this period may be gained from a contemporary document which described the threat to the social order that Gypsies represented and justified the penalties imposed:

One shire alone is sure at one time to have these Egyptian lice swarming within it, for, like flocks of wild geese, they will ever fly one after another ...

The cabins where these land pirates lodge in the night are the out-barns of farmers, in some poor village or other, who dare not deny them for fear they should, ere morning, have their thatched houses burning about their ears ...

These barns are the beds of incest, whoredoms, adulteries and of all the other black and deeply-damned impieties; here grows the cursed tree of bastardy; here are written all the books of all blasphemies ...

These are those Egyptian grasshoppers that eat up the fruits of the earth and destroy the poor cornfields ...

To sweep those swarms out of this Kingdom there are no other means but the sharpness of the most infamous and basest kind of punishment. (quoted in Judges, 1965)

But despite this sequence of laws and the apparent finality of the remedies they propounded, the resilience of those they attacked must have been quite remarkable. Regular statutes were tabled throughout the 18th and early 19th centuries, and with the increased urbanisation of the industrial revolution they were frequently cited as Acts against rogues and vagabonds or hawkers and peddlers. An Act of 1810 required the licensing of such folk and was followed in 1822 by a consolidating measure, the Vagrancy Act, which retained most of the earlier provisions. In the same year the Turnpike Roads Act imposed a fine of 40s on any Gypsy encamping on the side of a turnpike.

In the early 19th century, Gypsies come into view through the literature of the era; we catch glimpses of the drama they represented in rural life, in the works of George Eliot, Jane Austen and Sir Walter Scott. In *Emma*, Harriet is accosted and threatened by Gypsy children and is rescued, fainting, by Frank Churchill. And in Sir Walter Scott's *Guy Mannering*, there is a poignant episode when the laird, Mr Bertram, deliberately avoids being present at the eviction from his land of a Gypsy band; but then, by chance, meets them in a lane as they retreat. He is berated by a young Gypsy woman Meg Merilies:

Ride your ways Godfrey Bertram! What do ye glower after our folk for? Theres thirty younder, from the auld wife of a hundred, to the babe that was born last week, that ye had turned out of their bits of bields, to sleep on the moors! Ride your ways!

Under George IV, in 1824, a stronger vagrancy measure was aimed specifically at anyone pretending to tell fortunes by palmistry, or otherwise to deceive; anyone "wandering abroad and lodging under any tent or cart, not having any visible means of subsistence, and not giving a good account of himself" was liable to three months in prison. However, it removed the special reward offered in the previous measure to constables who apprehended a vagrant.

As industrialisation and urbanisation spread across the land, a further series of Public Health Acts, Highways Acts, a Commons Act and measures against peddlers and vagrants all contained specific clauses directed against Gypsies. Local authorities were empowered to control stopping on commons, and to regulate hop-picking and casual farm labour. Even the seminal Housing of the Working Classes Act of 1885 applied controls on "nuisances in tents and vans" to which new bye-laws were directed.

In 1889, the year county councils were created, infectious disease controls and sanitary provisions were directed at caravans. Local councils were given powers in 1899 to regulate commons and in 1908 a Children Act enforced compulsory education for travelling children.

The advent of the 20th century saw no let-up in the stream of parliamentary and bye-law legislation which was either directly aimed at travelling people or which, as a consequence of wider intent, encompassed caravan dwellers within its provisions. Thus the Children and Young Persons Act 1933 and the Public Health Act 1936 could be used against the way of life traditionally experienced by Travellers.

For example, the 1936 Public Health Act was essentially designed to attack overcrowding in slum dwellings, but included a clause enabling tents, vans and similar structures to be classed as a statutory nuisance if prejudicial to the health of inmates or giving rise to nuisance.

Post-war Town and Country Planning Acts proved a crucial blow to the traditional, if hazardous, life which modern Gypsies had carved out for themselves and indirectly led to a radical new approach to the issues raised by a now growing population of Gypsies and other Travellers, and a developing political consciousness of 'civil rights'.

With a new Education Act in 1944 and new measures against litter, Highways Acts and Road Traffic Acts, it was becoming clear both to Gypsies themselves and to those in the settled population who sought to represent them, that some congruence had to be sought between a way of life that had not changed materially for 500 years and a society which urgently needed to plan more thoroughly for new and higher standards of urban and rural development, transportation, conservation and social development. The new welfare state was aiming at standards of support, personal health and subsistence which presented a real dilemma to any minority group which had traditionally stood outside, or on the edge of, the majority society.

We will examine in the next chapter, the hesitant moves toward a resolution of these issues, but any understanding of the process needs to be viewed against the historical backdrop which we have sketched above. It is perhaps possible to see society's response to the Gypsy phenomenon as of two kinds: reactive and proactive.

From the time of Henry VIII to the years after the Second World War, it was essentially reactive. Solomos (1989) argues that in reactive mode society feels the need to repress, to defend itself, to respond negatively at each stage, to those who reject its most fundamental tenets, whose instinctive behaviour falls outside the accepted norms. Laws at once reflect the prejudice and fear of the people and are seen to give strength both to the local and the national state, in coping with each new threat that emerges. Attempts in the mid-Victorian period, by George Smith of Coalville (whose activities are discussed in Chapter 2), to introduce a more positive, proactive approach, were firmly put down (Smith, 1880).

Thus, from the early direct threats to the person, whether by beheading or by expulsion, the sanction moves to attacks on the culture; trespass, vagrancy and highways measures are supplemented by an attempt at evangelical work to assimilate Gypsies into the settled world.

It is only in the last 30 years, and specifically with the Caravan Sites and Control of Development Act 1960 that proactive responses emerge, and it is to that new era which we turn in the next chapter, arguing that it heralded a period of consensual, cooperative endeavour unique in the annals of public policy.

We need to trace in detail the incremental growth of policy and, with the aid of theoretical models of the policy process, to understand the nature and impetus to change, the stages of its development and the political and societal motivations which brought about the quite radical legislation of the 1960s.

two

THE ERA OF CONSENSUS: POLICY DEVELOPMENT FROM 1960 TO 1993

With hindsight, the decade of the 1960s was one in which new approaches to civil rights, to equal opportunities and to race relations legislation were given considerable emphasis. As part of that environment, the willingness to be proactive in dealing with the relationship of travelling people to settled society is quite marked.

It should be said that for perhaps 200 years the Gypsy cause had been supported from time to time both by their own occasional militancy and by individuals or groups who found either moral or romantic motivation in resisting the systematic intolerance and state oppression of itinerant people.

Acton (1974) argues that whilst in the Elizabethan era state racism took the form of expulsion and genocide, by Victorian times it had matured to an attitude of "sincere benevolence", though persecution remained just as harsh and straightforward. Knowledge about the Gypsies and a new romanticism reflected in the works of George Borrow and others generated a missionary zeal which produced both a manipulative benevolence and a continuation of the direct repression backed by the legal measures described in the previous chapter.

Acton demonstrates that most of this change of approach originates from the activities of one George Smith of Coalville, a mid 19th century brick-yard owner, philanthropist and eccentric, who, from a passionate religious conviction, agitated, wrote books and promoted various 'moveable dwellings' Bills and from whom, suggests Acton, most of the later lobbying stances have derived.

In post Second World War Britain there are perhaps three outstanding individuals whose activities have been important catalysts for change, and whose contributions to the formulation of policy have been crucial. They are Norman Dodds, a Kent MP, Ellen Wilmot-Ware, a west country tenant farmer, and Grattan Puxon, a radical activist whose work with Irish Travellers led to the foundation of the Gypsy Council, of which he was the first secretary.

It is significant that all three are, in Gypsy parlance, 'Gaujos' or non-Gypsies, and like so many other supporters, lobbyists and promoters of Gypsy civil rights their activities are grounded in the uneasy, ambivalent alliance between Gypsy people and their supporters which is a dominant theme of the modern Gypsy story. It is an alliance disfigured by tensions, spectacular quarrels, splits and reconciliation, in which there is never synergy or total harmony of purpose. However, without the work of Gaujos such as those mentioned above, it is unlikely that the public policy advances recorded here would have happened.

In post-war Britain government was facing massive problems of homelessness, reconstruction and economic regeneration. Pre-war legislation on public health, town and country planning, highways and housing were extensively revised. Issues such as mobile homes and caravan sites were not principally seen as Gypsy matters. Advocates for the interests of travelling people did not find it easy to be heard and were treated at best as eccentrics and at worst as agitators for a cause which seemed to have virtually nothing to recommend it.

Norman Dodds had concerned himself with the welfare of Gypsies since he was elected to parliament in 1945. There were extensive encampments along the Thames marshes and sprawling shanty towns in which the crudest facilities were either minimal or non-existent. His researches, parliamentary questions and lobbying, with the collaboration of an increasingly confident body of articulate Travellers, did much to progress the issues to the point where, between 1951 and 1953, the Ministry of Health and the Ministry of Housing and Local Government (MHLG) agreed to undertake a survey of the scale of the problems (Dodds, 1966).

Meanwhile a quite different campaign was being waged in deepest Gloucestershire. Miss Wilmot-Ware, a tenant farmer, had from the early years of the war allowed Gypsies to use her land. But when, with the aid of the 1947 Town and Country Planning Act, the local authorities began to prosecute and remove caravan dwellers from sites which were without planning consent or without business use, she found herself in direct conflict with the law.

Waging a passionate one-person campaign and fighting every legal action against her with a Christian martyr-like fervour, she rallied the highest levels of the church, MPs and other public figures to bring to public attention the injustice and oppression which she witnessed. Although her personal crusade was ultimately unsuccessful and all but destroyed her, there is little doubt that its longer-term effects were significant (Acton, 1974; Dodds, 1966).

By the early 1960s, Gypsies and Travellers were beginning to find a voice of their own and to organise what Acton calls a "self-sufficient and self-directing" Gypsy movement. It was a movement tinged with militancy, linked to international movements and to evangelical pressure groups, and, like so many movements of its kind, had a tendency to split asunder in bitter internecine dispute and rivalry.

The leading protagonist in this field was Grattan Puxon, a radical, not to say revolutionary young journalist, whose charismatic and articulate personality was pivotal to the success and continuity which eventually produced the Gypsy Council. With a base among Irish Travellers and early experience in the passionate politics of Dublin and its itinerant issues, and with an administrative efficiency not previously encountered by the British bureaucracy, Puxon led the first truly national campaign which was genuinely the voice of the Gypsies and Travellers themselves.

Thus it is possible to discern, at the very least, a three-pronged movement towards a post-war consensus on the need to produce policies which met the needs of this minority, misunderstood and widely feared group. Whilst Dodds worked patiently at the level of constitutional reform, Wilmot-Ware campaigned in open defiance and resistance to the existing law, fighting through the courts and marshalling the voice of the establishment wherever she could bring it to her aid. Puxon, by contrast, organised the Travellers themselves, ready to meet discrimination with militant resistance and to issue manifestos of defiant rhetoric reminiscent of the Bolshevik revolution.

This is not to suggest that these were the only voices raised in support at this period. Bodies such as the National Council for Civil Liberties, writers such as Brian Vesey-Fitzgerald, and numerous individuals of academic or church-based motivation, were supported by a few professional local government officers who could see that whatever the public reaction to Travellers, some kind of rational policy response was essential.

The opposition too was consistently vocal, bitterly opposed to any concession, whether on settled sites or the provision of other services. The most persistent expression of these views tended to come from bodies such as the Rural District Councils Association, the National Farmers Union and organisations of professional planners. Whilst it is difficult to recreate the spirit of this period, we can begin to discern a movement towards the later environment in which positive, proactive policies could emerge. 'At the very least', the collective conscience seemed to say, 'let us find out just how much of a problem we have here'.

A number of highly publicised evictions of groups of Travellers occurred in the late 1950s and the need for yet tighter planning controls prompted a review of the much larger problem of residential caravan sites. Fuelled partly by the post-war housing shortages, the growth in mobile home ownership had risen by 1959 to over 150,000 and was the subject of an official report in that year which did not consider the issue of itinerant Travellers. It led to the passing of the Caravan Sites and Control of Development Act 1960. This measure, which had not been primarily concerned with Gypsies and Travellers at all, nevertheless had major implications for them. It provided powers to control the unlicensed setting up of sites and sanctioned district councils to prohibit caravans on commons. Councils could issue licences and there were powers to provide new sites for Gypsies. The Act also allowed exemptions from the need for a licence for short stays, for seasonal workers on farms and for various commercial purposes.

The effect was to reduce rapidly the number of sites available for stopping, and many Gypsies who had earlier bought their own land and established a site found themselves unable to get a licence without a valid planning consent, and were therefore facing eviction. Their plight became the subject of continuous national publicity, conflict and debate to the extent that Dodds could characterise it as having become "charged with dynamite". In a debate in the House of Commons in December 1961 he reviewed the conditions of Travellers throughout Europe and concluded that the condition of Gypsies in England and Wales was "the worst in the world" (Hansard, 1961).

Dodds pleaded for national action rather than local initiatives, and urged that sites of up to 50 or 100 caravans with educational provision and basic amenities be planned on a national basis. The government's response was one of sympathetic understanding, but an insistence that, with the discretionary powers now provided in the 1960 Act, it was for local authorities to decide what measures were required and to act accordingly. Nevertheless this parliamentary occasion did much to publicise the issues and was the high point in a long campaign in which Dodds not only kept the problems alive, but gradually won the confidence of many travelling people.

The combination of the practical effects of the 1960 Act and the publicity gained from the debate in the House of Commons in December 1961 persuaded the minister of housing and local government to issue a circular (6/62) to all local authorities urging them to carry out surveys and to start sites. Government assistance was also offered.

Dodds was also told privately that the ministry would do all it could to encourage councils to make provision and following the ministry circular, plans were made in Kent, Surrey, Hampshire and Hertfordshire which, over time, developed into a slow trickle of official caravan sites. By 1967 the ministry could report that 14 sites were in being.

A more significant move came following the election of a Labour government in 1964, when the minister, now Richard Crossman, supported his officials' proposal to carry out a comprehensive national survey of the Gypsy population, their geographical distribution and their social and economic condition.

It was undertaken with the involvement of local authorities in March 1965 and became the basis for a seminal document published subsequently as *Gypsies and other Travellers* (MHLG, 1967). It was upon the findings of this report that all subsequent legislation and action at the time ensued. Whilst, with hindsight, many commentators have come to believe that the statistical count which was the basis of the work was vastly understated, it was nevertheless the first scientifically-based attempt to measure the Gypsy population.

The report's description of the living conditions, economic activity, and the social attitudes that Gypsies faced, set in the rapidly changing environment of 1960s Britain, represented a penetrating analysis of the plight of an unregarded minority group and made a case for immediate action to free Gypsies and Travellers from official harassment and deprivation. It also predicted that the Gypsy population would double in size in 20 years.

The survey had located 3,400 Traveller families in England and Wales, made up of about 15,000 individuals, but the authors themselves felt this represented an under-estimate of the true figure. It nevertheless became, in due course, the basis for site provision nation-wide.

Crossman had been convinced, within two months of taking office, that national action was required. In his diary for December 1964 he records having met councillors from Kent, where new sites were being constructed but were attracting large numbers of Gypsies from all over the country as a result. "I discovered the Gypsy is now becoming a serious problem on a national scale. It's obvious that something will have to be done nationally" (Crossman, 1977).

For the government, facing an increasingly militant Gypsy Council and yet more repression and evictions by local authorities, it was clear that exhortation by circular was not producing sites in the numbers required. The chance came in 1967 to move policy forward when a private member's Bill, promoted by the liberal MP Eric Lubbock, proposed a mandatory duty on authorities to provide sites. With significant changes, including a provision to grant exemption or 'designation' for counties and cities which had reached a target number of sites, the Act became law in the summer of 1968 and came into force a year later.

The 1968 Act thus became, and has remained for 25 years, the foundation upon which all subsequent interaction between Gypsies and the state has been posited. It has enabled other issues to be progressed, other services to be planned and has provided the basis for measuring progress - or the lack of it - ever since, giving a legitimacy to the arguments, disputes and confrontations which inevitably continued at every level, from the House of Commons and council chambers, to the roadsides and encampments in towns and villages throughout the country.

In a real sense the Act meant that Gypsies had 'arrived' in as meaningful a way as when they first appeared in the villages and towns of 16th century England. This is not to say that the Caravan Sites Act 1968 was a panacea. It was, in fact, flawed and inadequate; it was ignored by recalcitrant authorities and by unenthusiastic ministers.

The Act imposed a duty on county authorities and London boroughs to provide sufficient sites to meet the numbers of Gypsies and Travellers residing in or resorting to the area. However, in London and the county boroughs only 15 plots per borough were required. It provided a definition of what is meant by the term

'Gypsies and Travellers', and it provided for the financing of sites through the normal borrowing mechanisms of local authorities.

The district councils in each county were to be responsible for the management of sites, once established. No time limit for fulfilling this duty was prescribed and the secretary of state was empowered to arbitrate in cases of dispute between counties and districts, and to direct an authority to make provision in the event of failure to comply.

The definition of travelling people covered by the Act was as follows: "Persons of nomadic habit of life, whatever their race or origin" but it goes on to exclude travelling showmen and circus people and was specifically devised as 'non-ethnic', but rather attempted to define a way of life (DoE, 1985).

The provision for designation of areas which had made site provision sufficient to satisfy the secretary of state, meant that in such 'designated' areas Travellers would commit a criminal offence if they camped on unauthorised land. As will be seen from Figure 1, this provision meant that in due course vast tracts of England and Wales eventually became 'no-go' areas, and that although the numbers of sites provided country-wide fell well below the requirement, the areas in which they could legitimately travel were reducing incrementally.

Many felt that designation was a 'carrot', to encourage authorities to make the minimum possible provision; and it quickly became characterised as discriminatory and penal, targeted uniquely against those the Act was meant to assist. By design or not, the designation provisions in part II of the Act had the effect of criminalising one minority group, legitimising a prejudice into the very structure of the instrument created to alleviate the discrimination that Gypsies and Travellers had suffered down the ages (Hawes, 1987).

Theoretical considerations

It is as well to pause at this point and to give some consideration to the theoretical framework in which this story of developing policy is to be grounded.

**Figure 1: Designated areas of England and Wales, under section 12
of the Caravan Sites Act 1968, February 1988**

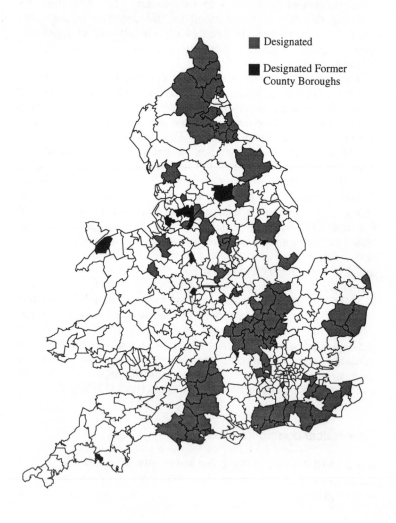

For those whose main concern is to implement policies and to be concerned with the practical problems which arise, it may perhaps be helpful to attempt to give meaning to the way in which the 1968 Act and the subsequent actions occurred. A necessary prior step is to seek an appropriate model of policy making; to examine a variety of approaches to the theorisation of the way policy gets made, and to select one which could facilitate understanding of policy making as process.

In the context of this discussion it is helpful to relate the concept of political decision making taking place within a system, to the description of policy making as a process, both of which take place within a social and economic environment rather than simply as the detached activity of remote and disinterested decision makers.

Academic interest in the last 50 years has been concerned with both prescriptive and descriptive propositions: in other words how should it happen and how does it happen? Writers in the tradition of Simon (1958) have proposed relying upon rational means of isolating objectives and selecting the most appropriate means to secure the chosen ones. In later work, Simon and others have proposed to 'satisfice'; that is, to accept that what is theoretically ideal may not be possible in practice, for lack of resources or information, and therefore to accept that the central concern of administrative theory should be with the boundary between the rational and the non-rational, or realistic aspects of human and social behaviour - with 'bounded rationality'.

Simon also suggests that policy makers are limited by the values, conceptions of purpose, habits and reflexes of the individual who can respond in rational terms to the policy goals, only to the extent that he or she is able, informed and can comprehend. Only within the bounds laid down by these factors are his or her choices rational and goal-oriented (Simon, 1958, p 241). This is an especially important point when related to the making of policy in a field as sensitive as provision for Gypsies. The question then, as Hogwood and Gunn pose it, is "how would policies be made if we were all capable of perfect rationality?" (1984, p 44).

Contrasting with these notions, adherents of other descriptive models apply what Allison (1971) has called a 'conceptual lens' through which we view our activity and try to make sense of it. Writers such as Lindblom (1959) dilute the importance of rationality in favour of the idea of "successive limited comparisons". In other words, whilst the starting point for thinking about a policy may be to ask what is the logical solution, the reality is that it is necessary to accept that the existing situation exists and that it has to be the starting point for policy development, which will then change in a series of small, incremental steps. Thus the test of success is not whether the policy is logically the best, but whether it secures the broad agreement of all the interests involved; something more likely to be achieved in small steps forward rather than by a grand new plan which starts from scratch.

Lindblom argues that incrementalism, or 'muddling through', is both a good description of how most policies are actually made, and a model for how they should be made. To muddle through more effectively is better than to aim for some super-human comprehensiveness.

For the purposes of this volume, what is of interest is the emergence of policy on provision for Gypsies and Travellers, as a step-by-step process, growing out of the interaction among a widespread range of participants. These include local authorities, professionals, Gypsy activists and supporters, ministers and local residents, all of whom have influenced the way policy has emerged.

It is argued here that only by analysing the incremental nature of the process might it be possible to pin-point the way in which the latent hostility and prejudice which surrounds the subject becomes built in to the very legislative structures meant to offer solutions to the issue which generates the hostility.

The ideas of Hogwood and Gunn (1984) provide an appropriate tool for this task. They also have, in common with other writers mentioned above, the concept of cyclical renewal or 'succession', complementing the political system model. Hogwood and Gunn propose a mixed framework for the analysis of policy which has as its defining characteristic a prescriptive aspect, a bias towards the improvement of policy processes. It is 'mixed' in a number of senses. First, it can be used for both prescription and description and, second, it does not conform rigidly to either the rational or the incremental notions discussed above. Hogwood and Gunn's model is not so much a middle way as a recognition that the appropriate mode of analysis will depend upon the issue and the context. Finally, it is mixed in that it is concerned both with the application of techniques for analysis and also political process. The process is envisaged in nine stages thus:

1.   deciding to decide (issue search or agenda-setting);

2.   deciding how to decide (issue filtration);

3.　issue definition;

4.　forecasting;

5.　setting objectives or priorities;

6.　options analysis;

7.　policy implementation, monitoring and control;

8.　evaluation and review;

9.　policy maintenance, succession or termination.

These are the stages through which an issue may pass, although the authors stress that this will not happen in every case; rather the stages constitute a framework for organising an understanding of what may happen or not happen. The process may be truncated or perhaps re-ordered and the dividing lines between one stage and another may be blurred.

The difficulty for analysts is to bring some semblance of order to the disaggregated manner in which policy is initiated, processed and shaped in the complex environment of British government, and indeed to ask whether or not any idea of coordinated or rational policy formation may be a myth. Hogwood (1987), in a later work, builds on the theoretical framework discussed here and sets out to chart the emergence of policy in practice, allowing issues to surface and become shaped by institutions, groups and key actors. He suggests there is no one way of characterising or defining public policy, but, for the purposes of this book, the influences which are at work in the field of Gypsy policy may be more readily understandable by utilising his cyclical concept.

In using this approach in the particular context of site provision it is necessary to avoid a too slavish devotion to the well-organised, yet essentially idealistic and atheoretical model and to make two modifications to the Hogwood and Gunn thesis. First, a tenth stage must be added to the list: that of 'feedback', to recognise that the outcomes of policy frequently do - and in the case in point certainly have - caused repercussions or renewal of the cycle of activity. Second, and in order to illustrate more readily the cyclical nature of public policy formation, the concept must be shown in circular form (see Figure 2).

With this framework in mind it is now easier to dissect the stages of development of policies emerging from the DoE between 1960 and 1994, and also the responses provoked in the fields of education and health, insofar as they addressed the lifestyles and problems of the Gypsies and Travellers on the roads of England and Wales.

Figure 2: A model of the policy process

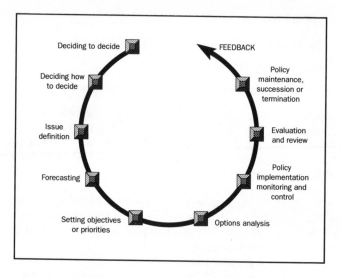

Source: Hawes (1993, p 54)

The 1968 Act in operation

There is a sense in which the 1968 Act represented an attempt at the 'rational' model of policy formation, in that the approach had been to research the scale of the problem, via the research undertaken by Adams et al (MHLG, 1967), to go back to basics and to start afresh.

The Act had proposed a comprehensive solution in which authorities would assess total needs and make the necessary sites available.   It is clear from the speeches and ministerial pronouncements accompanying the Act that it was seen by its creators as a once-and-for-all, complete package to solve the problems, after which there would be no further need for action.

The reason it failed to be comprehensive was more to do with flaws in the approach and implementation than in any weakness of rationality; the policy was defective in three respects.   First, the initial assessment of numbers and needs was, with hindsig lamentably under-estimated; second, the Act is concerned with site provision only, disregarding issues of social provision; and third, it failed to set a time-scale within which the mandatory duty to provide sites was to be completed.

As we shall see, with in-built weaknesses of this magnitude, the 1968 Act quickly became not a rational, comprehensive, once-and-for-all solution to a minor but pressing social problem, but instead a very early incremental stage in a policy saga that still has no end in sight and arouses more partisan passions 30 years on than it did at its inception.

Given the hostility to Gypsies which existed at the time the Act was introduced, and the failure of political will of successive governments since then, there are aspects of the Act's implementation which reflect the latent prejudice of society generally towards the putative beneficiaries of the legislation.

The provision for 'designation' of counties and London boroughs, referred to above, was uniquely prejudicial to the Gypsy lifestyle and in London it was possible for a borough to achieve designation having provided only 15 pitches. Of the 32 authorities, 28 have done so resulting, in practice, in almost the whole of the metropolis becoming a 'no-go' area for all travelling people, apart from the small percentage lucky enough to have a pitch, from which, not surprisingly, they seldom move (DoE, 1991c). The parallels with 'ethnic cleansing' of Balkan cities in the recent wars is not so very far-fetched as all that.

Another extraordinary outcome is the failure of successive secretaries of state to use the powers provided to them in the Act to direct recalcitrant authorities to make provision. In cases where local reluctance or opposition had resulted in no sites being created, it is the fact that the minister made no attempt to use his powers until, in 1977, court of appeal decisions in favour of Travellers had the effect of forcing the DoE to take this power seriously.

It is remarkable, and virtually without parallel, that a mandatory duty imposed by parliament can be ignored for nearly 30 years by a large number of local authorities; that the government could view this with equanimity for so long is an indication of the weakness of the Act in that it can reflect the latent prejudice of public opinion on the issue.

It is, however, true that there have been a number of attempts at evaluation and review in the intervening years. The Act became fully operational in 1970, and after five years of operation it was

that it was not providing the swift and
on which had been foreseen. John Silkin,
and local government, said:

parent that the rate of site provision is
ate. In consequence, unauthorised
encampments continue to proliferate in most areas, with all
that they mean in terms of nuisance, public health hazards,
community tension and law enforcement problems, as well as
misery for the Gypsies themselves who live under constant
threat of eviction. (DoE, 1976a)

By the end of 1976, there were only 133 sites in existence,
including temporary and permanent ones, offering 2,131 pitches in
all. But 20% of these had been in existence before the Act came
into force (DoE circular 28/77).

Significantly, by this time 13 London boroughs had been
designated, having provided the 15 pitches required; 10 former
county boroughs had been designated as having made adequate
provision; 2 more London boroughs had been exempted on grounds
that no provision was necessary, as had a further 26 former county
boroughs (DoE circular 28/77).

The government's response was to commission a detailed review
of the working of the Act, its effectiveness and the financial and
administrative arrangements for its implementation. It also sought a
review of the provisions for exemption and designation. Mr John
Cripps was appointed to carry out this review and he published his
conclusions in December 1976 (DoE, 1976b).

The Cripps Report

Cripps commented upon the sporadic violence and confrontation
which had occurred between Gypsies and the settled population
since the Act's inception, but set it against the relatively minor scale
of the problem. He pointed out that it ought to be possible, in
England and Wales, with a joint population of over 49 million, to
provide legal settlements for a minority group of less than 50,000.
But in a thorough-going review of the issues, he was able to pin-
point some of the inherent weaknesses in the legislation.

At this point the intention of policy was clearly to support the
concept of nomadism and the rights of people to live in caravans; as

Cripps points out, a 1969 development control policy note is explicit on this point:

> [The Gypsies] need, unlike that of the settled population, is for caravan sites, not houses. The secretaries of state have no wish to deny Gypsies the right to a nomadic existence. (DoE, 1969)

But he questions the estimated size of the Gypsy population and provides an alternative estimate, suggesting that those quoted in the 1967 research (3,400 families consisting of 15,000 people) is, in reality, more like 8,000 to 9,000 families, or 40,000 people - and growing. On this basis, the government's estimate that 200 sites would be needed (MHLG circular 49/68) was, argued Cripps, likely to increase by at least a further 300 sites.

In analysing the reasons why, after more than five years of a mandatory duty, local authorities had not responded to the duty to provide sites, and less than a quarter of the level of provision had been achieved, Cripps suggested a number of underlying problems.

The sheer pressure of public opposition to suggested sites is the most obvious reason and, he commented, it is not possible to overstate the intensity of feeling "bordering on the frenetic" aroused by a proposal to establish a site in almost any reasonable location.

He cited the tendency to criticise Gypsy habits, beliefs about their tendency to be aggressive to the settled residents, the rise in petty crime associated with their arrival, and the range of problems caused by untethered animals and the unruliness of young children, as part of the difficulty of establishing sites.

Cripps also reported a tendency to vandalism on sites which had been set up, suggesting that site design, the avoidance of communal facilities and consultation with Travellers on locations, were important issues to be considered.

In a wide-ranging series of recommendations to improve the effectiveness of the 1968 Act, the Cripps report was a significant stage in the policy life-cycle, reviewing the implementation of the Act at a point when it seemed palpably to be failing. In presenting it to the secretary of state, John Cripps was emphatic about the short-comings he found:

> My enquiries to date have convinced me that the growing shortage of places where Gypsies can stop lawfully, and the slow rate of official site provision are aggravating the already

severe tensions between house-dwellers and Gypsies to the point where the risk of outbreaks of violence is very real. I see very little prospect of improvement under present arrangements. (DoE, 1976b)

The recommendations urged a greater commitment by government to the purposes of the Act, with the same priority being given to sites as to council houses. The proposals included financing the capital cost of sites directly by the Exchequer, local authority assistance to Travellers to buy their own land, the sale of surplus government land for sites and a quota to be laid down for each authority.

Other recommendations included the appointment of Gypsy liaison officers by county councils, the location of sites to be more reasonable for the requirements of Gypsies and more consultation with Gypsy organisations. The report also suggested that a range of provision, including emergency, temporary and transit sites, should supplement those built to more permanent standards.

Government was urged to do more research into Gypsies' and Travellers' needs, to set deadlines for local authorities and to prevent the harassment and eviction of families whilst the site provision programme was under way. The secretary of state was invited to use his powers of direction against recalcitrant councils and to give up his power to grant exemption to authorities. Existing exemptions should be withdrawn. It also suggested that a national advisory body, to include Gypsy members, should be set up.

The response: circulars 28/77 and 57/78

There can be little doubt that the impact of the Cripps Report was significant; in the period following its publication, there were a series of actions from Whitehall which included two lengthy circulars of policy advice, a new Act and the setting up of a new division within the DoE, headed by a principal officer.

In particular, circular 28/77 (issued before government had made firm decisions on the Cripps Report) made an important attempt to meet the strictures it contained; it advised local authorities to make a wider range of sites available, to consider temporary and emergency stopping places during the process of providing permanent sites, and gave advice on easing the planning procedures.

The rules about designation were tightened, making it potentially less easy to achieve; there was a clear reiteration of the view that the Gypsy way of life was one which was valid in its own right, and should be valued and respected for itself - a statement of principle first made a decade previously.

The circular also urged a relaxation in eviction and harassment of families parked on illegal sites, until full provision had been made, and sought to get authorities to take account of the domestic and social consequences of forced removal before taking action. The circular encouraged a sympathetic and flexible approach to planning applications from Travellers themselves; it suggested that they should be allowed to set up with minimal facilities initially, that farm sites should not automatically be refused and that the licensing of sites should be "adapted to circumstances".

Subsequently, circular 57/78 formally presented the Cripps Report's recommendations with the government's response, confirming the 100% grant and clearly indicating the acceptance of the need for a high priority for the Gypsy sites programme.

The debate at this point in the development of policy illuminates the inherent paradoxes and conflicts existing within, on the one hand, the thrust of planning policy and, on the other, the impetus to official site provision.

Planning, as Home (1984) points out, seeks to define the right to use land through planning consents, policies and zoning, and established use; but the Gypsy way of life does not easily fit into these concepts.

Occasional, seasonal and intermittent use, a variable mixture of activities, a mix of residential, work and storage usage, are all part of the travelling culture. A site in the Gypsy life might be expected to be home, stable for the horses, yard for the domestic animals and workshop. It will need to be a parking space for caravan, car and lorry and might be the base for re-processing waste in one season, a macadam dump in another, and scrap metal sorting shed in another.

This is the normal and 'valid' way of life which on the one hand circular 28/77 urged should be respected, but which on the other makes nonsense of the zoning policies inherent in the town and country planning legislation.

Another, at first unspoken inconsistency is that if Gypsies, encouraged to settle on sites and even provide their own, begin to spend most of their time in one place, do they cease to become itinerant? Do they then no longer meet the definition of Travellers set down in the 1968 Act?

Local authorities have argued that if Gypsies have "strong local connections" and a more or less permanent base, they are then insufficiently nomadic to be regarded as Gypsies any more. If it is argued that they do not have strong local connections, then they are not entitled to be considered for housing (Home, 1984).

No doubt the urging, in circular 28/77, of a "flexible and sympathetic approach" was an attempt to meet these anomalies, but it does nothing to recognise that they are examples of a cultural prejudice or presumption of a norm, which militates against a different style of existence.

The Local Government, Planning and Land Act 1980

The new impetus engendered by Cripps was continued in the 1980 Act in which there were five further important modifications of policy, most of which flowed directly from his report.

The key change was the introduction of grant from the DoE (presaged in circular 57/78) towards the capital cost of site construction, releasing authorities at once from the arid argument that they could never get enough political priority to expend their own stretched capital allocation on Travellers when faced with many other pressing needs. The expenditure nevertheless still ranked as part of the block-grant allocation and had to be assessed as part of an authority's overall spending priorities. In the three years following its introduction, grant expenditure increased nearly three-fold, as shown in Table 1.

The increase in pitches was equally promising: by January 1983 there were 3,295 pitches on 207 sites run by local authorities, representing an estimated 42% of the total provision required (HC 414, 1985). However there were 3,910 caravans counted on those pitches suggesting a degree of doubling up of at least 18%. Home (1984) estimates that at this point nearly 1,000 new pitches were the direct result of the 1980 legislation, costing, on average, £10,000 each (see Table 2a).

The Act also ended the secretary of state's powers to exempt authorities from providing sites, as Cripps had proposed, and removed the need for site licences to be issued by county councils for their own schemes, a bureaucratic barrier which had not helped the earlier programme.

Table 1:   **Annual capital expenditure on site provision in English authorities, 1979/80 to 1993/94**

Year	Outturn (£m)	Year	Outturn (£m)
1979/80	£1.4	1987/88	£4.4
1980/81	£2.0	1988/89	£5.8
1981/82	£3.6	1989/90	£5.4
1982/83	£1.8	1990/91	£7.1
1983/84	£2.0	1991/92	£8.8
1984/85	£3.6	1992/93	£12.3
1985/86	£5.0	1993/94	£12.8
1986/87	£5.3		

Source: DoE, Gypsy sites branch, July 1994

Note: The total for Welsh authorities to end 1993/94 = £6.1m

However, the local authority lobby won a significant argument on the 'designation' issue. Whereas Cripps had resisted the suggestion that designation should be granted to district councils who had a site, whether or not the county as a whole had reached the required number of sites, the new Act introduced this change, on the grounds that it would encourage individual districts to get on with the task of providing sites and assisting counties to find suitable land in their areas, with the prospect of designation once the site was established. To reinforce the point, the 'sting in the tail' for Travellers was that the powers to remove illegally parked vans within designated areas were increased.

By one measure at least, this strategy has been a success; following the 1980 Act, 15 districts in England had been designated by April 1983, together with a further county and two London boroughs. In the first three years of the Act's measures, the number of Gypsy caravans on unauthorised land in England went down from 49.8% to 42.3%, mirroring the increase in council sites (HC 414, 1985).

The new measures were accompanied by pressures on local authorities to devise time-limited programmes and to appoint specialist liaison officers to coordinate action throughout county areas.

The improvements in the effectiveness of implementation did little, however, to lessen the political battle which continued to rage whenever a particular site location was proposed. Frequently, counties and districts were in conflict, and sites identified by county officers were vehemently opposed by district councillors and local residents. These constraints, added to the tight spending controls of the time, still left considerable implementation issues for local politicians.

Whilst the arguments concerning designation had been a constant theme throughout the period of the 1968 Act, there is demonstrable evidence that, once offered to district council level authorities, its propensity as a 'carrot' to encourage local action has been (together with the offer of grant aid) salutary. The increase in site numbers in the early 1980s is testimony to that fact. But it is, at the same time, at the heart of the argument about discrimination and prejudice. Designation provides a clear legal sanction, uniquely applied to Gypsies and Travellers, which has the effect of criminalising a way of life. In a designated area it becomes an offence to station a caravan for the purpose of residing for any period:

- on land within the boundaries of a highway;

- on any other unoccupied land;

- on any occupied land, without the owner's consent.

And since most areas which have achieved designation have done so in return for a minimum acceptable level of pitches, it follows logically, and if taken to its extreme, that the whole of England and Wales could become prohibited to Travellers who have no legal stopping place. By the end of the 1980s the numbers of Travellers were increasing faster than pitch provision, so the possibility of a completely designated country, short of the number of pitches needed, is by no means far-fetched.

The ethical point to stress is that this element of the legislation, in the interests of the settled majority, restricts the rights of a minority culture, to the extent that it threatens not only a way of life, but the very existence of the Travellers altogether. It is of no consolation to Gypsy families that authorities are exhorted to a 'compassionate' approach to action under designation powers, nor does it mitigate the discriminatory nature of the Act.

This raises another, more subtle contradiction in the underlying policy stance of government. It has been noted above that in circulars and statements, the DoE has stressed the validity of the Gypsy culture and has urged that it be respected for itself. But at the same time, for example in guidance to planning authorities on development control, there is an explicit suggestion that in due course, they will all settle into conventional domesticity, in houses, and will assimilate into the settled population.

Development Control Policy Note no 8, puts it plainly:

> The first need is to provide an adequate number of properly equipped sites on which Gypsies can live in decent conditions and where they can be encouraged to settle down and send their children to school. ... Eventually, of course, they may move into houses, but the majority are not yet fitted or willing to do so. (DoE, 1969)

Policy research in the 1980s

The impetus provided by the 1980 Act was boosted from time to time by a series of documents issuing from government on a range of aspects of Gypsy provision. In addition to circulars advising on implementation, there were a number of influential documents aimed at local authority practitioners which had the effect of inching policy forward in an incremental way which should not be overlooked.

Site management

The relatively new skills required to manage the emerging sites were encouraged in *The management of local authority Gypsy sites* by McGill, who researched best practice in 1982 (DoE, 1982). This gave advice on practical issues, including the allocation of pitches, maintenance, site regulations, rental and other payments. It also advised on the approach to policy and council organisational structure, but counselled against the growth of a 'Gypsy industry' or large bureaucratic structure. Instead it advocated self-help and much consultation of travelling people in the setting up of facilities.

Also in 1982, the DoE commissioned a study of the needs of long-distance Travellers, many of them Irish, whose activities had begun to cause some concern to local authorities. These groups typically travel in large groups of 50 or more caravans dealing in tarmacadam work, carpet sales or scrap. They travel throughout the country, stopping in an area for perhaps a month, before moving on to another location.

Normal council sites, already full, provide no opportunity to stop legally with the result that there is an inevitable occupation of land such as playing fields, car-parks or factory sites and, in most cases, very considerable disturbance and protest from local people. Such groups typically re-visit a location only once in three or four years. By 1980 it had become evident that the programme of sites envisaged in the 1968 Act had no relevance to the needs of these long-distance Travellers, and that it was a different phenomenon, requiring quite other solutions.

The study by Smith, Gmelch and Gmelch (1982) recommended that a series of "serviced stopping places" be provided, located along the main motorway networks and that more emphasis be given to transit sites with limited planning permission and limited facilities.   It was clear from this work that the programme of establishing local authority sites of the conventional kind had little relevance to the small but highly-charged issues raised by these nomads. Whilst this report was generally welcomed, it has not so far resulted in any action or any recommendations to local authorities.

The Environment Select Committee

By 1985 the impetus provided to the programme of new sites by the 1980 Act had waned and the annual increase in provision was minimal. The House of Commons Environment Select Committee, in reviewing the annual estimates of the DoE, was surprised to find a budget head of £5 million for Gypsy sites and began an inquiry into the effectiveness of the policy.

It became clear from the bi-annual count of English authorities that there were still over 3,500 caravans illegally parked or without proper stopping places, and that, on current counts, this represented about 35% of the total numbers (see Table 2a). Whilst the Welsh figures show some fluctuation in the numbers of caravans, the sites available remained virtually consistent throughout the ten years between 1985 and 1994. There were 40 unauthorised encampments in 1985 and 41 in 1994; these contained 284 caravans in 1985 and 280 in 1994. Even local authority provided sites increased by only 5 (from 17 to 22) in that period, allowing the number of caravans accommodated to increase from 370 to 419. However, the contribution made by private sites reduced by nearly 50% (see Table 2b).

It is, however, important to be clear about the statistics which are utilised in the debate about Gypsies, the figures used in measuring progress and the estimates of growth in the travelling population. The twice-yearly count undertaken by local authorities and published by the DoE is of the numbers of caravans on both public and private sites, and on unauthorised stopping places. The occasional publication of numbers of sites in being refers, in most cases, to both publicly-funded and privately-owned sites. But it is not always made clear what the relationship is between numbers of sites and levels of individual pitches they comprise. Table 3 attempts this in regard to council sites but does not make the same analysis for privately-owned ones.

The demographic picture is even more prone to uncertainty since, of course, many families have more than one caravan; on some sites a pitch will contain two or three caravans, and the national census data on family size is limited by the inevitable problems of capturing personal details of constantly moving itinerant households. These factors, and the regular non-response of some authorities in the bi-annual count, make the task of measuring real performance a hazardous one for DoE policy makers.

As a result, the Environment Committee recommended that the time was ripe for a 'modest review' of the effectiveness of the policy, pointing out once more that it comprised a mandatory duty on local authorities, that it was a relatively minor programme for which resources had been provided, and that still, 15 years on, the matter had not been resolved (HC 414, 1985). In a debate in the House of Commons in July 1985, the chair of the Environment Committee, Sir Hugh Rossi, said: "I hope that the minister will look into this much neglected area of his department's responsibilities" (Hansard, 1985).

The government's response was swift and sympathetic; a wide consultation followed, in which local authorities and others, including Traveller support groups, were invited to comment and to offer suggestions for ways to speed up and modify current policy. It was acknowledged that the major inhibition to new sites was "the concern of local people and businesses about almost any proposal for the development of a Gypsy site" (DoE, 1985).

Table 2a: Counts of Gypsy caravans in England, 1979-94

Date	Caravans on authorised sites						Caravans on unauthorised sites		Total
	Public	%	Private	%	Total	%	Total	%	
Jan 1979	2988	35.7	1194	14.3	4182	50.0	4176	50.0	83?
Jul 1979	2472	29.7	1262	11.9	3734	44.8	4601	55.2	83?
Jan 1980	3031	35.5	1252	14.7	4283	50.2	4245	49.8	85?
Jul 1980	2992	33.5	1185	13.3	4177	46.7	4760	53.3	89.
Jan 1981	3433	38.1	1369	15.2	4802	53.3	4211	46.7	90?
Jul 1981	3035	34.8	1233	14.1	4268	49.0	4449	51.0	87
Jan 1982	3506	39.6	1595	18.0	5101	57.7	3742	42.3	88?
Jul 1982	3365	37.1	1258	13.9	4623	50.9	4453	49.1	90?
Jan 1983	3910	42.1	1448	15.6	5358	57.6	3940	42.4	92?
Jul 1983	3555	38.9	1651	18.0	5206	56.9	3943	43.1	91?
Jan 1984	4416	44.5	1632	16.4	6048	60.9	3881	39.1	99?
Jul 1984	3913	40.6	1748	18.2	5661	58.8	3966	40.8	96?
Jan 1985*	4570	46.0	1893	19.1	6463	65.1	3472	34.9	99?
Jul 1985	4008	42.2	1678	17.7	5686	59.9	3810	40.1	94?
Jan 1986	4766	45.0	2022	19.1	6788	64.1	3804	35.9	105?
Jul 1986	4467	42.9	1793	17.2	6260	60.1	4156	39.9	104
Jan 1987	4740	45.0	2181	20.7	6921	65.7	3614	34.3	105?
Jul 1987	4461	42.0	2073	19.5	6534	61.6	4075	38.4	106?
Jan 1988	4931	45.6	2339	21.6	7270	67.2	3546	32.8	108?
Jul 1988	4546	41.5	2139	19.5	6685	61.1	4265	38.9	109?
Jan 1989	5159	45.6	2422	21.4	7581	67.0	3740	33.0	113?
Jul 1989	4789	44.5	2104	19.5	6896	64.0	3884	36.0	107?
Jan 1990	5199	45.0	2471	21.4	7670	66.4	3874	33.6	115?
Jul 1990	4922	41.1	2435	20.3	7357	61.5	4610	38.5	119?
Jan 1991	5469	45.4	2704	22.4	8173	67.8	3877	32.2	120?
Jul 1991	5035	40.9	2609	21.2	7644	62.1	4672	37.9	123
Jan 1992	5494	43.0	2959	23.2	8453	66.2	4324	33.8	127?
Jul 1992	5065	40.4	2713	21.7	7778	62.1	4754	37.9	†125?
Jan 1993	5876	44.5	3139	23.8	9015	68.3	4183	31.7	131?
Jul 1993	5432	42.4	2976	23.2	8408	65.6	4402	34.4	‡128?
Jan 1994	5951	45.5	3271	25.1	9222	70.6	3838	29.4	#130?

Notes: *   Adjusted using Jan 1984 figures for 29 returns not received.
          †   31 authorities did not make a return.
          ‡   7 authorities did not make a return and the July 1992 return for carava?
             on council sites has been used. Of these authorities, 4 had notified the?
             DoE that no return could be made due to the non-availability of transp?
             because of an industrial dispute. 3 further authorities were only able t?
             supply partial information due to the industrial dispute.
          #   2 authorities did not make a return.

Source: DoE, Prepared 13 April 1994

Table 2b: Counts of Gypsy caravans in Wales, 1985-94

Date	Caravans on authorised sites					Caravans on unauthorised sites		Total
	Public	%	Private	%	Total	Total	%	
Jan 1985	370	51.6	62	8.6	432	284	39.6	716
Jul 1985	342	51.3	45	6.75	387	279	41.9	666
Jan 1986	334	55.8	43	7.2	377	222	37.0	599
Jul 1986	Figures not available							
Jan 1987	403	60.0	26	3.5	429	247	36.5	676
Jul 1987	385	57.5	25	3.8	410	260	38.7	670
Jan 1988	303	59.3	13	2.5	316	195	38.2	511*
Jul 1988	355	54.0	62	9.0	417	244	37.0	661
Jan 1989	405	62.0	64	10.0	469	186	28.0	655
Jul 1989	419	62.6	24	3.6	443	226	33.8	669
Jan 1990	-	-	-	-	471	182	27.9	653*
Jul 1990	386	57.3	53	7.8	439	234	34.7	673
Jan 1991	476	68.8	26	3.76	502	189	27.5	691
Jul 1991	425	60.0	18	2.5	443	265	37.5	708
Jan 1992	431	61.5	37	5.3	468	232	33.2	700
Jul 1992	-	-	-	-	283	226	44.4	509*
Jan 1993	404	61.5	24	3.65	428	228	34.8	656
Jul 1993	288	46.2	69	11.0	357	267	42.8	624*
Jan 1994	419	57.0	35	4.75	454	280	38.2	734

Note: * Incomplete returns

Source: The Welsh Office, July 1994

Table 3: The relationship of local authority site provision to numbers of new pitches, 1988-93

	Sites	Pitches
Jan 1988	258	4267
Jan 1989	268	4518
Jan 1990	275	4614
Jan 1991	283	4766
Jan 1992	286	4828
Jan 1993	301	5021

Source: ACERT

Following a large and mainly critical response, the secretary of state, Nicholas Ridley, commissioned the Emeritus Professor of Countryside Planning at London University, Dr Gerald Wibberley, to analyse the responses. From his subsequent report (DoE, 1986), a series of proposals were adopted, to boost the site development programme. These included:

● stronger pressure on recalcitrant councils;

● tighter control on designation;

● more accurate annual counts;

● a strengthened Gypsy sites branch at the DoE;

● a new attempt to clarify definition of Travellers;

● encouragement of offers of permanent housing;

● encouragement of private sites;

● speed-up of grant application approvals;

● more emphasis on providing transit sites.

The Wibberley Report had itself attempted a new definition of who qualified as Gypsies or Travellers under the 1968 Act, an issue which is discussed in a later chapter; but it is significant that, for the first time, the issue of other kinds of Traveller, and especially the so-called New Age groups, was raised: "Many Travellers or 'itinerants' such as so-called 'peace' convoys and summer 'pop' festivals, will fall outside the Act and those problems will have to be dealt with by other means" (DoE, 1986).

It is evident at this point in the incremental development of Gypsy policy that there is an inherent, cross-party consensus at national level about the need to press forward with the site provision programme. In debates in the Commons, in statements by ministers and shadow ministers, despite widely differing views about the Gypsies themselves, it is generally agreed that the programme must go on and provision must be made. This is not to say that the matter was considered one of great priority. Indeed it is acknowledged that it is a brief which is given to the most junior of junior ministers, and is not a matter from which electoral success is ever likely to be extracted.

In contrast, no such consensus exists at the local level. At the community level, where political decisions and those who make them are much closer to the voters who will be affected, the hostility to making Gypsy sites available is frank and explicit. Even among those party politicians whose ideological bent predisposes them to help minority groups and the disadvantaged, the public utterances are at best ambivalent. The tension between meeting a mandatory duty and responding to the prejudices of local voters is palpable.

It is only when some large and disruptive outbreak of unofficial parking occurs, causing inconvenience and visual dereliction, that many local people will come face to face with the human and social problems of providing for a minority way of life, with no obvious or immediate solutions.

It is in this context, in the town halls and meeting rooms of Britain, in protest meetings and consultative enquiries, that the average member of the public addresses the problem with a degree of rational contemplation. And in these circumstances, the possibility of rehousing into permanent homes is a frequent issue for debate.

The Wibberley report had suggested that perhaps 250 Gypsy families moved into permanent housing in 1985, whilst another 100 moved out. Thus the contribution which this possibility offers is small but significant. However, in order to analyse this trend, the DoE's own research division undertook a survey which argued that conventional housing might make an increasing contribution to the Gypsy accommodation problem. It suggested that changing lifestyles among the travelling people themselves, the loss of the rural itinerant employment pattern and a wish to educate children in settled schools, might tend to fuel the drift to conventional domesticity (DoE, 1987).

The survey, conducted among 50% of the English local authorities, showed that 84 Gypsy families had been rehoused from official sites in 1985; a further 112 had moved from illegal sites. However, 67 families who had been housed previously moved back onto the road, giving a net 'gain' of 129. On the assumption that similar trends operated in the remaining districts, the survey concluded that 250 families moved in and 100 moved out, during the year. Thus, if between 200 and 300 families are getting pitches on council sites each year, and a further 100 are providing their own private pitches, the contribution which rehousing can make is significant.

But the factors which influence families in making these major decisions about their future lifestyle, indicate that there are both 'push' factors and 'pull' factors.

The DoE survey found that the important 'pull' influences were the wish to educate children in stable school environments, the wish of older Travellers to settle down, the need for access to medical facilities, and the awareness by some families that other relatives had achieved the transition happily.

Influences tending to 'push' Travellers into housing included the inability to get onto a still scarce supply of sites, the growth in family size, family feuds, poverty, including the inability of some Travellers to replace worn-out vehicles, and the wish to avoid harsh winter conditions and tightening eviction regimes.

An important factor to emerge from this survey is that nearly 30% of all Travellers who go into settled housing move out within five years, a statistic which demonstrates vividly that as a mechanism for 'solving' the Gypsy problem, it has little relevance, beyond perhaps offering an alternative choice of lifestyle for a minority of traditional travelling people. To establish rehousing as an important part of the overall policy response to Gypsy accommodation needs is perhaps to reinforce the thought that the ultimate aim of policy is to make the travelling life disappear altogether.

Evaluation and review: I

At this stage in the life-cycle of the policy encompassed in the 1968 Act, it is perhaps worth re-capping on the strengths and weaknesses of the measure. By the beginning of 1988, the DoE believed that the Act had secured 65% of the site provision required, with about 3,314 pitches in being on 276 council sites. There were 110 designation orders covering one-third of district councils in England and Wales (see Figure 1). The minister had used his powers of direction against Hertfordshire and Surrey, as well as against two Welsh authorities. He had sent warning letters to both Hereford and Worcester, and Avon, threatening the use of directional powers if site provision was not stepped up (DoE, 1991c).

Most commentators and parliamentarians at this point felt that, given the relatively small size of the issue and the length of time it had taken, these performance levels represented a degree of failure. For the student of the policy process it is perhaps worth pausing

Critique of the '68 Act.

once more to consider the causes of the undoubted implementation gap.

With hindsight it is possible to see more clearly the flawed nature of the Act itself. There are perhaps eight immediate weaknesses in either the structure of the legislation or the implementation, which can be said to have weakened the 'top-down' aspects and reinforced the reluctance of authorities to provide any 'bottom-up' impetus to action.

- There is an inherent failure to recognise the differing constituencies and circumstances - the difference between the pressures on London boroughs, rural areas, and metropolitan cities. Similarly the Act makes no differentiation between the various needs of Gypsies and Travellers, between long-distance groups and local families.

- The model of provision and management, giving a cumbersome split between the role of county councils (to identify land and construct sites), and the districts (to manage sites) has led to conflict and lack of cohesion at local level.

- The unsatisfactory nature of the financial provision, with a 100% grant, but counted against overall capital allocation, has meant that Gypsy site spending has had to compete against other, more popular priorities for annual spending estimates.

- The inadequate basis of knowledge about both the numbers of Travellers needing sites, and about the demographic trends within the travelling community, has led to uncertainty and lack of positive targets for authorities.

- The 1968 Act, solely concerned with providing sites, appeared unrelated to the need for other measures concerning health, education and welfare services for families once allocated pitches - an issue taken up in later chapters of this book.

- The recognition of disadvantage, the ethnic dimension and other social policy issues were slow to emerge and did so in a way which militated against any coordinated policy approach.

- The designation policy was a device alien to the main thrust of the Act, representing a prejudicial and inherently anti-Traveller mechanism striking at the heart of any concept of respect and recognition of the validity of Gypsy culture. It was seen by authorities as a 'carrot' or prize for doing the minimum it was possible to get away with, and the minister's failure to use his directional powers until quite late in the process reinforced that understanding.

- There was little political impetus behind the Act, from any party, either locally or nationally, beyond occasional exhortations to act more quickly.

The growing awareness of these problems by the end of the 1980s had been assisted by an increased tendency of the Travellers and their advocates to use the courts in their arguments with both government and local authorities. As the next stage in the policy process unfolds, and yet another Act of parliament is brought forward, it becomes evident that, as a DoE source has put it: "Ministers are increasingly aware of the role of the courts in shaping their actions" (quoted in Hawes, 1988).

The role of the courts

A curious feature in the history of the 1968 Act has been the extent to which the courts have intervened in its implementation, shored up its weaknesses and shaped outcomes. Unlike almost any other social measure of its kind, the Act's propensity to be driven forward by judges rather than politicians is a measure both of its inherent weaknesses discussed above and of the fatal stratum of prejudice lacing its overt and practical intention to provide legitimate sites for itinerant people.

Gypsies have increasingly been willing to resort to judicial review as a way of challenging local authority inaction. Judicial review has burgeoned in recent years as more and more citizens feel able to challenge the decisions of government agencies and local authorities, and local government attempts to challenge central government.

The concept, enshrined in administrative law in 1977 by order 53 of the rules of the supreme court, ensures that the infringement of the rights of the individual by the administrative decisions of legally empowered authorities can be remedied without resort to the costly processes of writ (Boynton, 1986). If it can be shown that decisions were either wrong in law, illegal or were irrational or unreasonable, or that they were made via procedural impropriety, the citizen can seek judicial review and the individual can be assured of fair treatment.

The concern of some legal administrators, that this process leads to the possibility that judges control government, has not prevented courts from intervening in a wide and diverse range of issues (Feldman, 1988). As Boynton (1986) comments, judicial review is a growth industry.

In a sense, the use by Gypsies of these legal mechanisms in order to obtain legal stopping places, suggests the idea that 'political' rather than 'legal' redress is being sought against administrative inaction - a concept which Ridley suggests is deeply embedded in British political traditions and has imprinted itself on British ways of thought (Ridley, 1984).

There are two issues on which high court and appeal court judgements have contributed important interventions. The first is in the matter of the reluctance of local authorities to fulfil mandatory duties and the almost equal reluctance of secretaries of state to use their powers to direct them. It is possible, in tracing the progress of court interventions, to discern a strengthening of resolve and a bolder use of judicial overview as time went on.

The second issue relates to the problem of defining which groups of travelling people come under the Act; this surfaced somewhat later, as new kinds of Travellers began to feature more prominently, both on the roads and in the media.

Since the Act did not specify any timetable for provision, the slow progress made placed many Gypsies in an intolerable position, being moved on whenever they stopped illegally, but having no legal place to go. By 1974 many had begun to challenge particular local authorities in order to clarify their legal rights.

As the DoE's own research has shown, early decisions were not always favourable towards Gypsies (DoE, 1991c). In *Kensington and Chelsea LBC* v *Wells*, the judge held that an authority was not in breach of its duty to provide sites unless or until the minister had directed it to do so. This view was upheld by *R* v *Secretary of State for Wales, ex parte Price* in 1984, but an important turning point came in the same year when, in another case, (in re Ward), the applicant requested the secretary of state to direct a borough, which he declined to do. The applicant then sought judicial review which was granted, setting a precedent that an individual Gypsy has 'sufficient interest' in the circumstances to apply for such a review. The verdict of the review was that the Act requires local authorities to make provision "irrespective of whether or not the minister has exercised his power to give directions" (DoE, 1991c).

The Ward decision was rapidly followed by the case of *R* v *Secretary of State for the Environment, ex parte Lee.* Mr Lee applied for judicial review on the grounds that the county council concerned had failed to make site provision, and that the secretary of state had improperly failed to direct it to do so. The judge found in favour of Mr Lee and the secretary of state's decision was overturned because, in considering the request for directions to be given, he had misrepresented the law.

The seminal case, however, was *R* v *Secretary of State for Wales and West Glamorgan County Council, ex parte Gilhaney*, in 1986. The county had been unsuccessful in its attempts to provide sites and effectively had discontinued its efforts. A group of Gypsies camped illegally, and the council was determined to evict them. The council's decision to evict was quashed by the court on the grounds of its failure properly to address its duty to provide sites.

In summary, it was clear that government was under increasing pressure from the courts to take firm measures against councils which had not complied with statutory duties imposed on them. Furthermore, the option of judicial review could be utilised by complainants, who might be individual Gypsies, to examine the actions or lack of them, on the part of local authorities or even the minister (DoE, 1991c).

Gypsies and the planning system

The other network of legislation which has within it both attempts to accommodate Gypsies and at the same time the weapons of prejudice, is that comprising the Town and Country Planning Act of 1947 and its subsequent amendments, directives, guidance and development plan policies.

Todd and Clark (DoE, 1991c) have reviewed in detail the impact of planning law on Traveller policy and have commented that despite ministerial exhortation, support for a sympathetic approach towards private site applications is still rare.

The framework for local land use planning has been provided by development plans required under a series of town and country planning Acts in 1947, 1967, 1971 and 1984. County structure plans provide a broad indication of intended development patterns, the details of which are provided in district or local plans. Home (1987) indicated that whilst some structure plans contain specific approaches towards Gypsy sites, often advocating that they may be considered as exceptions to green belt or other restrictive settlement policies, other plans make no mention of the subject.

In many districts, local plans provide evidence of the prevalence of what Todd and Clark call "indifference or hostility" to the need for Gypsy sites - and to the statutory obligation to provide them. It is not unusual for districts to state unequivocally that no such site can be located in their area.

If actual or proposed developments fall outside the scope of land use specified in development plans, the relevant local authority can take action to remove or prevent such a breach. Proposed developments can be refused planning permission. For existing structures, the local planning authority can serve an enforcement notice where it appears to them that a breach of control has been committed.

The procedures first fixed under the 1947 Act still broadly exist. Importantly for Gypsies, the Act allowed the retrospective permission for sites set up without consent and this has enabled many families to remain on land first settled without permission, and to apply for permission later.

Many have found that, having established good relations with neighbours, there is little opposition once a consent is sought. Others, however, having bought land and sought later approval, have risked enforcement proceedings, fines and even an injunction and sale of their land.

Hyman (1988) noted that even if Gypsies are aware of the illegality of using their land for setting up home, the only alternative, camping on the roadside, is also illegal. By occupying their own land they gain respite, can sometimes make the process lengthy and also have the chance, at least, of winning their case.

DoE statistics (DoE, 1991c) suggest, however, that the refusal rate for Gypsies who have sought permission for private sites is as high as 90%, with a marginally better result on appeals against refusal. But planning appeals are costly, lengthy and bureaucratic. It is in the light of such statistics, perhaps, that the secretary of state issued circular 28/77, urging a sympathetic and flexible approach to such applications "in order to encourage self-help among Travellers". In a subsequent circular (57/78) he said, "it would be to everyone's advantage if as many Gypsies as possible were enabled to find their own accommodation".

It would appear that the value of private sites, in the overall site provision strategy, has been given more broad support by planning inspectors than by district council planning committees, given the differing success rates of initial applications and subsequent appeals.

Furthermore, in some instances, inspectors have specifically referred to the inadequate numbers of sites within a local authority area as a factor in allowing private site appeals (DoE, 1991c).

The Local Government and Housing Act 1989

In 1989 in the Local Government and Housing Act, a further boost to the programme came with a new form of capital grant for local authorities, which provided for reimbursement of the capital cost of building sites, no longer counting against the overall capital allocation of the authority. This quickly became known as the 'golden grant' and was designed to remove the element of competition which such projects faced when set against other spending priorities in the annual programme of most local authorities.

Evaluation and review: II

Perhaps because of the increasing interest by Gypsy support organisations and civil liberties groups in the process of judicial review, there was in 1990 and 1991 a considerable further flurry of evaluation and review activity by the DoE. The Local Government and Housing Act having provided additional legislative impetus to the programme of site provision, there was an important debate in the House of Commons, and in 1991 no less than three new research publications on site provision policy.

These documents, thoroughly researched and offering a wide range of new advice both to government and the local authorities, covered virtually all aspects of Gypsy policy. Research on counting Gypsies, a good practice guide to site management and a review of policy were issued simultaneously (DoE, 1991a, 1991b, 1991c). The policy review, undertaken by W.S. Atkins and partners, was specific in its recommendations to make the legislation effective and urged a renewal of political will at both national and local level to complete the programme of site provision.

The debate in the House in July 1990 was another high profile step in the life of the 1968 Act. The Environment Select Committee once again brought the issue forward in its report on the

DoE estimates, providing MPs of all parties with an opportunity to complain of the slowness of site provision and the iniquities of continuing unofficial encampments.

It was a heated debate, noticeable for the underlying distaste and outspoken prejudice of many MPs for Gypsies and Travellers and their way of life. As often on these occasions, distinctions were made between the "respectable" Romanies and the irresponsible and reprehensible others, variously described as "Didecois" and as an "unsociable rabble". The designation powers were attacked as either inefficient or ill-used and government was urged to provide tougher sanctions, both against recalcitrant authorities and Gypsies stopping illegally. More resources were urged to enable the site provision programme to be completed.

In a reply, cut short by the time-limited procedures of the House of Commons, the parliamentary under-secretary indicated he was contemplating a threat to withhold the funding for sites from those councils who still did not produce site plans, with the implication that they would still be required to undertake the work, but at their own expense. In response to the Select Committee view that, at the current rate of progress, it would take 25 years to complete the programme, the minister, Mr Chope, admitted, "I take the realistic view that the problem will never be solved while we rely on the legislation we have" (Hansard, 1990).

Commentators at the time took this to mean that a new and more powerful Act might be brought forward. What actually occurred, within a few months of that statement, was profoundly and radically different; it was, in short, a proposal to scrap the Act altogether, to remove the duty to create new sites, and to introduce much tougher sanctions against Gypsies and Travellers who stopped illegally.

These proposals were linked with an intention to 'privatise' the whole procedure, making it clear that in future most new sites would have to be found and created by Gypsies themselves, using the same planning procedures open to any other developer or private house owner.

Termination: the end of the policy life-cycle?

As was explained at the beginning of this volume, the new approach was heralded in a pre-election press release from the Conservative central office during the June 1992 election campaign, and in a later chapter it is intended to examine the means by which the policy was refined and brought to fruition.

It will be necessary to ask what happened between July 1990 and June 1992. What new evidence or event, what new pressure had prompted the dramatic intention to wind up the 25 year old 1968 Act? It was a measure which, for all its short-comings, had provided a means of creating sites: a means which had the support of all political parties, of Travellers and their supporters, and even, in the last analysis, of those vociferous anti-Gypsy protesters so well represented by MPs in the 1990 Commons debate, who recognised that the provision of sites was better than the illegal encampments and might just be a way of finally persuading Travellers to disappear into the house-owning, settled and sedentary population.

However, before attempting to provide a commentary on the termination of this period of consensus over Gypsy matters, and to speculate on what will take its place, it is necessary to examine the progress since 1968 of allied social and welfare policy and the steps taken to provide education, health and child care services to the transient and mobile communities for whom the opportunity of a stopping place was now, slowly, becoming a reality.

We turn in the next chapter to examine the way in which a parallel public provision - that of the education service - has developed, and the contribution it has made to society's developing response to Gypsies and their families. This will trace the growth of education services for travelling children and the emergence of the concept of special provision as a complementary adjunct to the growth of legal sites.

three

THE DEVELOPMENT OF
EDUCATION POLICY

Following the introduction of the 1968 Caravan Sites Act, the primary thrust of government policy was to concentrate on increasing the provision of stopping places, but inevitably emphasis began to be placed upon complementary services. In particular, it became evident that provision would then have to be made for proper education and health care for the Travellers who would live on the new sites. The following pages will attempt to illuminate the growth of these services by tracing the development of policies aimed at meeting the educational needs of Traveller children, and examining legislation which has crucially affected their everyday lives, both before and subsequent to the 1968 Act.

This development can be divided into three stages:

- *the early years:*
  the early education and children Acts from 1902 to 1944 which were intended for the whole population but which failed to work for Traveller children, together with other social legislation which influenced Travellers' lives and consequently the education of their children;

- *the voluntary initiatives:*
  the work of the national and regional voluntary organisations in the 1960s and 1970s, especially in the organisation of summer schools which highlighted the educational deprivation of Traveller children and provided an impetus to local education authority provision;

- *multi-cultural education and a coordinated service:*
  the impact of moves towards a nationally coordinated programme together with the growing awareness of the need

for multi-cultural education leading to Her Majesty's Inspectorate (HMI) discussion paper *The education of Travellers' children, 1983*; The Swann Report (1985) *Education for all - the report of the Committee of Inquiry into the Education of Children from Ethnic Minority Groups*; and the 1988 Education Reform Act.

The early years

The law had recognised the need for educational provision for travelling children as early as the turn of this century, and since 1908 the children of Gypsies and other Travellers have been required (by law) to attend school for at least 200 of the normal 400 sessions a year. The root of this legislation was the Children Act 1908 which in practice, except in isolated cases, was never enforced. These issues are still under review as part of the Department for Education's guidance on policy and practice in relation to school attendance for all children and, in particular, the categorisation of absence.

Section 118 of the Children Act 1908 referred specifically to "vagrants". A study of the debates on the Bill in Hansard illustrates that ministers included Gypsies in the term although "they differed from other vagrants" (Hansard, 1908). Sub-sections 1 and 2 imposed a severe penalty upon parents who prevented children from receiving education. In addition to incurring a fine of 20 shillings, the parent also risked losing the child, who could be taken to "a place of safety", probably a certified industrial school. The Act gave power to "any constable who finds a person wandering from place to place and taking a child with him" to apprehend that person without a warrant. Sub-section 3 of section 118 made allowances for seasonal workers:

> ... this section shall not apply during the months of April to September inclusive, to any child whose parent or guardian is engaged in a trade or business of such a nature as to require him to travel from place to place, and who has obtained a certificate of having made not less than two hundred attendances at a public elementary school during the months of October to March immediately preceding ... (Children Act 1908)

Although included in the Act, the real target was not "Gypsies of the old kind" with whom the government on the whole sympathised, but the "vagrants", described during the debate as "the evil", whose way of life was considered by the government to be a serious threat to the settled society. It was apparent from the debates in parliament during the readings of both the Children Bill and the Moveable Dwelling Bill - a measure which subsequently failed to reach the Statute Book - that the government's underlying aim was to achieve the registration and social absorption of its wandering population. Earlier sections of the Children Bill had dealt with children found wandering and homeless who were leading a life of crime but were too young for imprisonment. The government proposed reformatory schools for the older children and industrial schools for the younger. Later, during the debate on section 118, it was made clear that caravan children could be included in those recommendations if necessary, but that the main purpose of section 118 was different in that its purpose was to penalise Traveller parents who deprived children of elementary education. Summing up, the home secretary described the Bills as "useful social legislation of a non-controversial kind" (Hansard, 1908).

Later that year, when the Children Bill passed to the House of Lords, the leader of the House, Earl Russell, moved the omission of the clause that eventually became section 118, considering the penalty too severe and the giving of such power to a police constable "unwise and dangerous". Earl Russell opposed the inclusion of Gypsies who, he said, were not opposed to education if it could be arranged in the winter months. He argued that "methods of conciliation rather than force would be more suitable" and that because Gypsies had great affection for their children, any attempts by a constable to enforce the removal of a child would "provoke a great deal of disorder, and probably lead to riot or bloodshed" (Hansard, 1908).

Although Earl Russell's amendment to remove section 118 was withdrawn, the House agreed to ask the Home Office to consider their concern. Acton argues that the intervention of Earl Russell, together with the informal intervention of Miss Dora Yates who was a member of the Gypsy Lore Society, led to the addition of sub-section 3, tagged on at the last minute to protect Gypsy and possibly fairground Travellers from wrongful arrest, provided that their children received education during the winter months (Acton, 1974). Although the Act was passed and section 118 was meant to ensure the education of Gypsy children even if part-time, it was not enforced and therefore had very little effect on Gypsies.

It was 25 years before further advances were made. The Children Act was amended by the Children and Young Person Act 1933 and later still by the Education Act 1944 so that the 200 attendances were required to be fulfilled over any period within twelve months rather than specifically over the winter months. This made no great difference, especially as this legislation and successive planning and public health Acts of the 1930s were later mainly used as a weapon to move Gypsies on.

Very little is recorded of schooling opportunities for Gypsy children in the decades following the First World War. The *Journal of the Gypsy Lore Society* mentions a local authority Gypsy school in a wooden chalet encampment in Hurtwood, Surrey in 1924.

School attendance officers visiting Gypsy sites may or may not have been aware that many Gypsies understood their role to be that of an unofficial eviction officer offering three choices - enforced education, payment of a fine for non-attendance, or moving on to avoid the first two alternatives - a 'no win' situation. For many travelling parents attendance of their children at school meant registration, which they thought might lead eventually to the removal of their children into care, or worse. Fraser (1993) comments that the fate of Gypsies in Europe at the time of the Second World War when, it is estimated, "from about a quarter of a million to half a million and more" Gypsies were massacred, had created an understandable fear and suspicion among them with regard to any kind of registration. Partly for this reason, many of them would hide their children during school attendance officer visits, thus avoiding registration, fine and eviction (Smith, 1984).

During the 1960s, as the debate about legal stopping places progressed, there was an increase in public concern regarding the educational neglect of Gypsy and Traveller children, influenced by the work of Norman Dodds MP, the founding of the Gypsy Council, and a number of government reports which highlighted the educational needs of the children. The continual movement of the majority of Gypsies at that time was caused mostly by the difficulty in finding a place to stop. For this reason, enrolling children at school was very low on their list of priorities. The Public Health Act 1936, the Town and Country Planning Act 1947, the Highways Act 1959 and the Caravan Sites and Control of Development Act 1960 were all used to prevent Gypsies from stopping, thus absolving local authorities from providing education or any other services.

The national survey of Gypsies which resulted in the publication of the government report *Gypsies and other Travellers* (MHLG, 1967) highlighted the extremely low numbers of children attending school and described the hardship faced by Gypsies. The research team recognised that the Gypsies were facing great changes in their lives, especially since the Second World War. Many were forced, because of advancing technology, to abandon their traditional crafts and occupations by which they earned a living. The report acknowledged that it was becoming increasingly difficult to stop in traditional camps, and added to this difficulty was the Caravan Sites Act 1960, which called for the licensing of caravan sites.

If there was any doubt about the validity of these claims, they were resoundingly confirmed by The Plowden Report, *Children and their primary schools,* which was published in 1967 and recommended that local education authorities should make a concerted effort to improve access to schools for Traveller children who were, the committee found, the most educationally deprived group in the country (DES, 1967). Many Gypsies too realised that they would need to adapt to the new legislation and became conscious of the need for literacy. Up to this point, policy advance had been inhibited by a two-fold resistance: the strong tradition of family-based education and informal educational development which had maintained Gypsy survival for centuries, and the lack of will from many education authorities. It is not perhaps surprising that progress had been so slow.

The 1967 MHLG report echoed the recommendations of the Plowden Report for more resources to be made available. Chapter 4 contained a study of the family and included a section on education. Although some of the contents would be considered patronising by today's standards in their reference to Gypsy children as "backward", "lacking stimulating experience" and "having a limited vocabulary", the report also clearly demonstrated a genuine concern for the plight of the travelling community. Its conclusion stressed that accommodation for Travellers was "essential". Its powerful argument was to form the basis of later legislation and laid the foundation for the policy on nomadism for the next quarter of a century:

The provision of sites or other accommodation for these families gives them amenities not otherwise available to

> them, not only domestic facilities, which the rest of the
> population take for granted, such as running water, electricity,
> drainage and sanitary facilities, but also schools, and health
> and welfare services ... perhaps the most important of all, the
> children are able to attend schools regularly. (MHLG, 1967)

In the event, however, the age of consensus was not without frustrations. Following the Caravan Sites Act 1968, it was thought that there would be permanent sites for Gypsies meaning that education in mainstream schools for the children would at last be possible. A few of the more responsible authorities had already taken initiatives for Traveller education, but progress was still extremely slow (many counties experiencing, or claiming that they were experiencing, financial difficulties) and very often influenced by the rate of permanent site provision which was non-existent in many areas.

The post-Plowden concern among teachers, local education authorities and the Department of Education and Science (DES) was for a common teaching approach and a coherent national response to the educational needs of Gypsy children. This included the need for better communication with travelling families, and an agreed teaching method which would be compatible with the new situation as more local authority residential sites came into being (Reiss, 1975).

Earlier work with the children of bargees and fairground workers had been partially successful, but had never overcome the mass lack of attendance of these groups. Research in 1976 suggested that between 10% and 15% of all travelling children actually attended schools.

In a complementary piece of research in 1973, the Schools Council had estimated that between 6,000 and 12,000 Gypsy children were of school age, and about 1,500 were known to be on school rolls.

Educational needs were shaped by the professionals, perhaps for the first time, against a growing awareness that Travellers are a highly distinctive social group with a complex but recognisably ancient heritage. It began to be publicly acknowledged that they are not merely "itinerant scrap dealers" or society's drop-outs (Reiss, 1975). In a report on the education of travelling children in 1975 the Schools Council said:

It is also a myth that they wish to abandon their lifestyle and settle. Rather, they are facing a crisis inevitably brought about by suburban development, shortage of wasteland and post-war legislation of planning and site licensing. Though genetically mixed, they are genealogically a close-knit and well-defined group with a unique lifestyle and value system. (quoted in Reiss, 1975)

As a result of a project launched by the Schools Council in 1976, it was estimated that the majority (perhaps 80%) are English or Welsh with a Romany-oriented cultural heritage, under 15% are Irish tinkers, found mainly in the North and Midlands, and the remainder are either Scottish (3-4%) or of mixed ancestry. This research also demonstrated that a small minority of settled Traveller families have attended school for generations; and in the 1960s and 1970s some schools serving sites established in the early 1960s had succeeded in establishing regular attendance, though this is less true at secondary level where premature adult status and early participation in the family economy conflict with schooling (Reiss, 1975).

Another clear tendency to emerge was that attendance declined sharply with advancing age once the secondary stage has been reached, although the desire for continued education, particularly literacy, might remain strong. The researchers concluded that participation by such adolescents in summer school programmes and in late afternoon and evening classes on sites meant that early release from compulsory day-time attendance could increase educational contact.

The philosophical issue for the teaching profession is to deal with the genuine dilemma over assimilation or pluralism. Many Traveller parents desire attendance by their children in the normal way and with no obvious differentiation in their treatment. Not all parents accept that a transition of preparation or 'bridging' into school is in the child's best interests. It was not always clear at this stage of the debate that decisions on the need for special measures should be a pragmatic response to a particular situation, rather than resulting from the predilections of teachers or administrators.

The practical dilemma, however, is that the socialisation of the Traveller child is almost exclusively within the family and kin-group. The child, therefore, moves only in a non-literate and unschooled circle. Solutions must obviously emerge from adaptation by both parties, but the initial burden of responsibility for change lies with schools and teachers, the professionals in the situation (Reiss, 1975). Much later, professionals working with Gypsy children wished to see their activities based upon more fundamental precepts. Members of the National Association of Teachers of Travellers (NATT) formulated their own beliefs in 1992 as follows:

> The following principles are fundamental to the aims, objectives and processes of education at every age, in every context and for every group. They should be evident and carefully monitored in *action* and *practice* throughout the education service.
>
> - A commitment to justice for all and equality of opportunity as a fundamental purpose and value.
>
> - A demonstration of the belief that society is strengthened and enriched by pluralism of background, culture, religion and perspective.
>
> - A recognition of the inequality of opportunity which exists within society for individuals and groups and a determination to take positive action to enable everyone to participate equally, to raise expectations and to enhance performance.
>
> - A commitment to question and counteract all forms of prejudice and discrimination.
>
> - An entitlement to quality, self-respect, respect for others, a broad and balanced education and a supportive environment as a basis for successful learning and participation.
>
> (The principles of the National Association of Teachers of Travellers, 1992)

It was not until the late 1970s, following the work of the voluntary organisations, the effect of HMI national overview and DES national and regional courses, that school provision for Gypsy and Traveller children began to improve.

The voluntary bodies

As so often is the case in British social policy, it was due to the hard work of the regional and national voluntary organisations in lobbying the government and local authorities, and in supporting and promoting education initiatives, that in the 1960s and 1970s urgently needed changes began to emerge. On-site caravan schools, run by Gypsy organisations and other charities, were initially welcomed by many Gypsies as the solution to more than one problem: they provided an education in which Gypsy parents could participate and which they could oversee; they were seen as useful as a staying process against eviction; and they might shame the government into providing proper sites and services. A flavour of the difficulties which faced those who undertook these activities can be gained from Acton's description of the setting up of the first Gypsy Council caravan school. He later wrote:

> In 1964 the first school put up by the Travellers' community and Grattan Puxon in Dublin was burned down by council workers. When the Gypsy Council was founded in England in 1966, the need for stopping places and the need for education were the two main points of its policy. The first Romano Drom (Gypsy Way) caravan school was opened in the summer of 1967 on the old Hornchurch Airfield in the London Borough of Havering. Some six weeks of pre-literacy and general language and number work, using both Romani and English, supported in part by a collection from the Gypsies themselves, followed. In September several of the children attended a state school for the first time in their life. At the same time, a fierce struggle took place to ensure that the Gypsies were not evicted from the old airfield but could stay to send their children to school. Eventually the leader of the Gypsies there became the first warden of a site in nearby Hainault. He also became the caretaker of the first permanent Gypsy school, run on Montessori principles by Venice Manley, who had been a teacher in the Dublin school which was burnt down. (Acton, 1974)

Many 'mobile schools' were set up during the 1960s and 1970s, mostly by voluntary bodies. Some education authorities followed this example by also providing mobile provision as a first step. At that time, the majority of local education authorities were still only offering the 'open door' policy, meaning that the schools were there for the children to use - let them use them. There were no plans to encourage and support the enrolment of Travellers. Some authorities provided mobile on-site provision in order to keep the children out of schools, and many Gypsies, concerned for the safety of their children, welcomed this action.

The work of national organisations such as the National Gypsy Education Council (NGEC) and the Advisory Committee for the Education of Romany and other Travellers (ACERT) was and still is invaluable, not only in campaigns to promote and support educational initiatives for Gypsies and Travellers but also in the work for equal access to accommodation, health and community services and in the elimination of discrimination.

The NGEC was set up in 1969, its main aim to make education available for the vast number of Gypsy children identified in the Plowden Report as receiving no schooling whatsoever (estimated to be 90% of the total). In the summer of 1971, the NGEC organised a national summer school project for Gypsy children for two weeks in August. The project was planned for both official and unofficial sites and its main aims were to provide initial and additional school experience for children as well as to promote liaison between the Gypsy community and the education authorities in order to resolve some of the difficulties already identified in the 1967 national survey. The project volunteers, half of whom were fully qualified teachers, made contact with over 200 families on 17 different locations in England.

The NGEC published a full report of the project and a follow-up conference was held early the following year in order to assess the educational response. They hoped that the summer schools would be seen as "catalysts in generating considerable interest and action towards providing educational facilities for Gypsy children" especially as local education authorities had been invited to visit project locations. The report makes it clear that those involved believed that: "the effect of the summer schools on the voluntary response was tremendous". In many cases, new Gypsy and Traveller liaison groups were formed following the end of the projects. Where existing liaison groups were asked to run projects, the activity brought a new sense of enthusiasm and direction to their efforts, together with the corresponding local support and goodwill (NGEC, 1971). These groups worked hard to nurture the interest and action that was triggered. The official response was encouraging.

Significantly, local authorities, who in the past had been uncomfortably slow regarding their statutory obligations to Gypsy and Traveller children, saw that practical and workable policies could be implemented. The report said: "There is, of course, little discredit in their apparent reluctance to cope with this particular problem. The pattern and tradition of social reform is one where initial response is of a voluntary character, followed by official recognition and support". The summer schools had taken a lead and local education authorities were particularly interested and had visited them. On both voluntary and official fronts, there had been a discernible, sharp upward curve in the amount of support and work for Gypsy education. The result of the summer school work must be considered as part of the success of the national projects: "In areas of great social deficiencies, the balance between satisfying ultimate and immediate needs is always a dilemma for decision makers, especially when there are grossly inadequate resources. It seems to us, however, that both these categories of demand were satisfactorily met in terms of resources available" (NGEC, 1971).

The NGEC has been superseded by the Gypsy Council for Education, Culture, Welfare and Civil Rights and continues to lobby the DES, now the Department for Education (DFE), and other educational establishments.

ACERT was established in 1973, with Lady Plowden DBE as its president. The organisation's first field officer later became a member of HMI, with eventual responsibility for the oversight of Traveller education in England. Because of ACERT's good relationship with the DES, it was able through its newsletter to inform local education authorities of early indications of governmental papers. It was unfortunate that the newsletter did not always get passed on to the teachers working in isolation on Traveller sites, because it also ran a regular feature, 'Regional Round-up', which updated authorities on increasing national provision and good practice (or lack of it). However, the feature provided an effective stimulus to those authorities which had previously made no provision at all for Traveller children.

Despite the good relationship with the DES, there were occasions when ACERT felt it was necessary publicly to voice its disapproval of some departmental action:

... following the refusal by the London Borough of Enfield to accept two Gypsy children presented for school by our field officer because the family was camped illegally, a decision has been handed down by the legal branch of the DES which could be read as saying that local education authorities do not have a responsibility to educate the children of roadside Travellers. This was a great shock to ACERT (and, we suspect, to the DES!) and, of course, it strikes at the roots of the work which ACERT is trying to do. Our chairman has written to the secretary of state, Mrs Shirley Williams, stressing our feelings that this decision negates much work which is being carried out by members of DES staff on behalf of Travellers and asking her to consider making changes in legislation placing a duty squarely on the shoulders of the local education authorities to educate *all* children, regardless of the legality of their parents' residence in their area. (ACERT, 1977)

As an example of ACERT's early work, in the summer of 1976, the honourable secretary organised a full summer school programme in Somerset and an action research programme in London. A mobile teaching unit was used for the research programme which was headed by two students from Dartington College who worked in close liaison with Tom Lee of the Romany Guild. The research was able to provide ACERT with valuable material which they later used in their approach to the Inner London Education Authority regarding the education of Gypsy children living on unofficial sites (ACERT, 1977).

Something of ACERT's style can be gleaned from its 1990s information leaflet: "ACERT makes information available to those requesting it and provides it to those who do not".

The 'no-area pool'

The amount of information both 'requested by' and 'provided to' local education authorities over the years, and especially during the 1970s, certainly influenced policy, sometimes directly and sometimes by chance. In December 1975, for example, Avon Education Authority wanted to increase its low base educational provision for Gypsies and Travellers but was unable to proceed because of financial constraints. In his response to the two part-time Travellers teachers' request to increase their part-time posts to full-time, the education officer for schools replied, "due to very severe financial restrictions, this is the very worst possible time for considering any increased financial commitment". However, four months later, the authority found enough money in the new budget to provide a suitably equipped van for the service. The field officer of ACERT was contacted for advice which resulted in negotiations and a subsequent letter from the DES:

> It has been agreed that the children of Travellers can be regarded as not belonging to the area of any authority, and that those authorities who provide services to meet the educational needs of such children should have their costs fully re-imbursed under the 'no-area' pooling arrangements. To achieve this, the relevant expenditure should be included in 'excluded services' on Form 512F (ie the form used to settle final audited claims).

It is not clear from the documents whether ACERT was ever aware of the indirect role it played in improving Avon's service for Travellers, but an article dealing with the 'no-area pool' funding appeared in ACERT's following newsletter:

> The pooling committee at the DES has finally made a decision about the use of the 'no-area recoupment pool' in relation to schemes for the education of travelling children. The basis has been changed but the principle is that claims can be made under certain conditions. We understand that the DES is soon to issue a circular giving a full explanation but if any local education authority or individual needs information before that time, if they would like to contact ACERT's field officer, she will be pleased to furnish them with a copy of the decision letter which has been sent to us. (ACERT, 1977)

It was not until 1989 that the DES produced a draft of the circular which eventually became circular 10/90. The 'pool' was originally organised under the Education (Miscellaneous Provisions) Acts 1948 and 1953, later regulated by section 32 of the Education Act 1980. It was available at the rate of 75% for teachers' salaries and 100% for resources for special provision for Travellers. It made a tremendous impact on the development of education policy, enabling authorities such as Avon to begin or enhance their services aimed at establishing links with Travellers and addressing their needs other than through the offer of the 'open door' policy - which for Travellers was no policy at all. During the late 1970s and early

1980s, more and more local authorities used the central 'pool' arrangements to finance coordinated provision. Lack of funding could no longer be used as an excuse for not providing educational support for Travellers.

However, despite the availability of financial support through the DES, many local authorities still did not claim, often because of the lack of political will to support any initiatives that might encourage Gypsies to stay in their area and often through a reluctance to shoulder the 25% contribution. There were, and still are in many areas, no votes to be won in local elections by providing sites and the related services for Travellers. The national organisations continued to campaign for changes in legislation and practice, and eventually, in the early 1970s, their policies received support from the DES.

The impact of coordination

A major turning point in Traveller education was the decision to introduce national coordination. In 1970 a member of HMI was given responsibility for the oversight of Gypsy/Traveller education, and in 1973 he organised the first DES short course on Gypsy/Traveller education. There were only 19 participants (as compared to the 250 course participants attending the courses in the late 1980s). The courses were held every other year until 1990, when they were discontinued, much to the regret of many people who worked with Travellers.

However, NATT, which sprang from a meeting of a small group of teachers at a DES course in 1980, continued to play an important part in the development of Traveller education and especially in the professional development of many teachers of Travellers. In 1992, NATT held its first conference which was supported by more than 40 local education authorities. It successfully provided continuity and established NATT as a professional support organisation sorely needed after the termination of the DES short courses.

In 1983, the long awaited HMI discussion paper, *The education of Travellers' children,* was published. It was a working document containing not only examples of good and bad practice, but also reminders regarding legislation, attitudes of local education authorities and Travellers which inhibit school attendance by Traveller children, recommendations for remedial action and details of government funding (DES, 1983).

The paper quoted numbers of Travellers in England, taken in a collated count in June 1982, as between 30,000 and 50,000, with accommodation on official sites for 37% with a further 14% living on private authorised sites. It estimated that there were between 12,000 and 15,000 Traveller children of school age in England and that probably as few as 40-50% of the primary-aged children attended school and of those only a few attended on a regular basis. The secondary-aged group was estimated as low as 10-15% registered in schools with attendance even lower.

Although the paper praised the efforts of voluntary groups, some local education authorities and schools, it highlighted the fact that "responses in some areas had been insufficiently sustained to establish regular school attendance as part of the Traveller way of life". The 'open door' policy was also criticised:

> In other areas poor practice can be identified by the operation of the 'open door' policy. The schools are there, so the policy goes, let the Travellers use them; that is if they remain long enough, are bold enough, confident enough, keen enough and persistent enough to seek and gain admission. It is not surprising that in these circumstances many fall at these hurdles, especially if there is an unacknowledged discrimination between those on official and those on unauthorised sites. (DES, 1983)

Networking which developed as a result of national and regional courses gradually ended the isolation of the teachers who were working in the field of Traveller education. It meant that interdisciplinary and interauthority consultation could take place. Local authorities could no longer use lack of information or lack of finances as an excuse for lack of educational provision, and in many areas it was this awareness that led to the development of other services.

In one county, the education authority set up extra 'bridging' provision to prepare a group of unofficially camped primary-aged Irish Traveller children for school. An annexe of an old school building was equipped, two teachers were provided and transport was supplied for the children. Six weeks into the project, the children failed to arrive and one of the teachers visited the site to find out why. The families had been evicted by the authority. In light of this incident, a representative of the education department was invited to be present at all county planning meetings concerning Travellers and the council included the following in its policy statement on the education of Travellers:

> Traveller education should be seen within the context of other services to Travellers, particularly in relation to site provision. The authority would seek to maintain continuous liaison with other departments concerned with the welfare of Travellers.

The county was thus forced to look not only at educational provision in relation to site proposals but also to look at site provision in relation to educational proposals.

1985 saw the publication of the Swann Report, *Education for all: the report of the Committee of Enquiry into the Education of Children from Ethnic Minority Groups*. The Swann Committee of Enquiry's brief was initially focused on children of Afro-Caribbean origin because there was a considerable number of them under-achieving in schools and a disproportionate number being placed in special schools. The report was also to prove a very important publication for Gypsies because although they were not to be recognised as an ethnic minority group until 1989, the Swann Committee decided that the group lay within their terms of reference and needed to be considered in the report. Swann placed Gypsies firmly within multi-cultural education:

> Whereas, with the other groups of children whom we have considered, we have been chiefly concerned with their needs *within* schools, many of the particular educational needs of Travellers' children arise because of difficulties in gaining access to the education system at all.

> In many ways the situation of Travellers' children in Britain today throws into stark relief many of the factors which influence the education of children from other ethnic minority groups - racism and discrimination, myths, stereotyping and misinformation, the inappropriateness and inflexibility of the education system and the need for better links between homes and schools and teachers and parents. (DES, 1985)

The Swann Report makes it clear that site provision is a central factor in considering the educational needs of Traveller children, and comments that while substantial numbers are forced to lead an unstable and unsettled existence it is difficult to discuss proper educational provision.

The fact that the Swann Committee of Enquiry came down in favour of provision being made within the mainstream system, and not separately, or on-site, or with peripatetic specialists, only reinforced the counter-productive nature of designation and 'no-go' areas, and the impossibility of parents having the right degree of security and peace of mind to contemplate sending children to school when they might face eviction at any time.

In West Sussex, for example, the county having achieved designation, the county secretary subsequently ruled that the education authority no longer had a duty to educate travelling children from unauthorised sites.

The authors of the Swann Report, however, recognised that simply having enough sites would not, of itself, provide for the educational needs of Gypsy children. It identifies the three broad approaches by local education authorities:

- *the open door policy*: no special provision or support; schools simply expecting Gypsy children to attend normal schools;

- *provision within schools*: special support within schools or in special units on the school site;

- *on-site provision*: special provision, by specialist teachers in units in mobile classrooms, on the Gypsy sites.

National bodies and local education authorities began to analyse and criticise the lengthy report. At the time, some members of the national organisations thought it was somewhat bland, containing nothing that could be used to combat racism or bring about change, but in a number of counties this proved not to be the case.

In the light of the Swann Report, many authorities made a positive response in appointing advisors for multi-cultural education whose responsibilities included oversight of Traveller education services. Other authorities, where multi-cultural education centres were already established, included the issues surrounding Traveller education in their development and equal opportunity and anti-racism policies.

The county of Avon provides an example of how identification of need by teachers, lobbying by national associations and DES recommendations (DES, 1983, 1985) led to the appropriate response to the needs of Traveller children by one authority. Avon, identified by the DoE as one of the recalcitrant councils regarding site provision, was also one of the many counties which, during the 1970s and early 1980s, provided only a minimum education service for Travellers, employing two peripatetic teachers working from a mobile classroom. The service was set up to provide a 'bridge' into schools for the children who were to live on Avon's first official site, due to open in 1976. Ten years later, in 1986, the mobile classroom was still operating a segregated service on that same site. The 'bridging' project had not been successful (see Chapter 4).

The two teachers, aware of a large number of unofficially camped families whose children were receiving no education whatsoever, had been lobbying the county's education officers at every opportunity to increase provision in light of the HMI discussion paper. After the publication of the Swann Report, the teachers renewed their efforts by identifying 297 Traveller children from the unofficial encampments and presenting the details of names, ages and location to a special support group, consisting of education committee members, heads of schools, advisor for multi-cultural education, senior education officer and head of multi-cultural education centre. This group had been set up by the authority to review the structure of the multi-cultural education centre. The support group was shocked that "a group of children, the size of a primary school had escaped their notice" and requested a full report of the situation by a senior education officer. At the same time, in the autumn of 1986, an opportunity presented itself to Lady Plowden, president of ACERT, to make Avon's new director of education as aware of the situation as she was. In addition, Avon Traveller Support Group lobbied the members of the county council to act regarding the education plight of the children.

In September 1987, Avon set up the Avon Traveller Education Group, a well resourced service consisting of eight teachers and ancillary support, with an office and resource base. A clear written policy was formulated regarding the education of Traveller children together with a transport policy. The service was funded by the 'no-area pool'. Chapter 4 will pursue the Avon story in more detail.

Following the Swann report, debates of this kind were raging in many county education departments, with varying outcomes. In 1986 at a short course in Chester, 35 teachers met to discuss professional needs and proposals for the future, which led to the publication, by NATT and ACERT, of the *Post-Chester proposals*. Despite nation-wide circulation, the response was very disappointing. A later questionnaire, circulated to all local authorities to discover how their policy and practice accorded with the proposals in the publication, indicated that there were still serious disparities in educational provision across the country. While Inner London and the West Midlands education services for Traveller children were operating well-established coordinated provision with other local education authorities, offering in-service courses and other general service facilities, many other authorities were only providing minimal support, very often a token service of one or two teachers working on Traveller sites. Some authorities still operate the 'open door' policy despite this being criticised in the DES discussion paper (DES, 1983), providing no support at all.

The Education Acts

The education system of England and Wales in the second half of the 20th century was established by the Education Act 1944. Section 36 of the Act expected parents to ensure that their children aged between five and sixteen years received efficient full-time education. There was an exception for those of a nomadic way of life in that the children should be registered at a school but needed to attend only 200 of the normal 400 sessions. The thinking behind this section aimed to protect Traveller parents from unfair prosecution, but many local education authorities used it to legitimise part-time education, or even a policy of inaction. Despite the recommendations of the Swann Report (DES, 1985) that this section of the 1944 Act should be amended, this was never done.

The belief of many was that the 1988 Education Reform Act eliminated this section by the introduction of the national curriculum which obliges local education authorities to ensure that all pupils receive full-time education and this means full-time attendance. This is not the case, however, and the 200 sessions section was still in place in 1994. In February 1994 the DFE produced a draft consultation paper, *School attendance - policy and practice on categorisation of absence*, which was circulated to all local education authorities and to a wide range of voluntary bodies, associations and unions. The secretary of state issued the final booklet in May 1994. Paragraphs 44-48 of the draft deals with Traveller children (DFE, 1994).

Despite the law, however, there are still many Traveller children who do not attend school regularly, and of those only a small percentage go on to secondary education and beyond. DFE figures taken from annual report returns 1990/91 and 1991/92 from the 75 local education authorities claiming section 210 funding in England, show that the number of Traveller children enrolments has risen by 8.87% (see Table 4).

Table 4:   Number of enrolments of Traveller children in 75 authorities in England, 1991-93

	Primary enrolments	Secondary enrolments	Total
1991/92	10,098	2,291	12,389
1992/93	10,826	2,672	13,498 (8.87% increase)

Source: DFE

DFE estimates indicated that the number of school-age Traveller children, residing in 92 of the 109 local education authorities in England, to be 19,700 compared with an estimate of between 12,000 and 15,000 ten years previously. On this basis a 68.5% enrolment rate is better than any earlier figure. However, these figures are only enrolments and do not indicate the number of actual school attendances, which are far more difficult to ascertain.

The reasons for this lack of school uptake have been debated for decades and meanwhile more and more Traveller children are becoming first generation school attenders. Many would argue that as one generation succeeds another and parents receive more information about education, so attendance at school will improve and the situation will thus resolve itself.

Others, including many Travellers, are not so optimistic and insist that the school attendance law should be enforced for Travellers as it is for the rest of the population. The problem facing many local authorities is how to enforce such a law when they have not provided the full quota of permanent sites as required by the 1968 Caravan Sites Act. They are well aware that lack of sufficient sites is the main reason for irregular school attendances among many Traveller children.

Under section 8 of the Education Act 1944, each local education authority has a duty:

to secure that there shall be available for their area sufficient schools

(a) for providing primary education and

(b) secondary education

and the schools available for an area shall not be deemed to be sufficient unless they are sufficient in number, character and equipment to afford for all pupils opportunities for education offering such variety of instruction and training as may be desirable in view of their different ages, abilities and aptitudes, and of the different periods for which they may be expected to remain at school including practical instruction and training appropriate to their respective need.

Some authorities thought that Travellers who were unofficially camped were not of 'their area' and, therefore, their duty under the terms of the Act would not apply. In 1977 the refusal of a school in Croydon to enrol a Traveller's child because her family was not living on an official site led to fierce protests by the NGEC and a threat to take the government to the European Court. Consequently, a clause was inserted in the Education Act 1980 to close the loophole. Paragraph 5 of DES circular 1/81 makes clear the right of Traveller children regarding school enrolment:

The reference to children 'in the area' of the authority means that each authority's duty extends to all children residing in their area, whether permanently or temporarily. The duty thus embraces in particular travelling children, including Gypsies.

The Education Act 1980 gave Traveller parents, along with all other parents, the right to state a preference for a particular school for their children and the right to appeal if they are turned down.

The Education Act 1981 gave parents of children with special educational needs the right to ask for and be involved in the assessment of their children under section 5 of the Act, so that suitable educational support is provided by the local education authority.

The Education Act 1986 meant that parents would be more involved with education through the appointment of school governors, and there would also be parent and pupil representation when school exclusions were considered.

The Education Reform Act 1988 caused a major change in the development of education generally, reducing the power of the local education authorities and clearly stating the entitlement of all children to a broad and balanced curriculum. With effect from April 1990, the 'no-area pool' funding for Travellers was replaced in England and Wales by a specific grant under section 210 of the Education Reform Act 1988. Funding was allocated to authorities in England from the DFE on the submission of a successful bid with particular emphasis on improving levels of enrolment and attendance and facilitating Traveller children's access to the national curriculum. Bids have to be made in advance, supported by detailed plans, and the grant provides 75% funding for the approved expenditure normally for a period of three years.

For authorities which had already been providing an education service for Traveller children, this marked the end of access to an apparently infinite source of money, the 'pool'. In England, 76 local education authorities submitted bids for 1990/91 to the DFE; 61 authorities were successful although 6 of these received only 20% of the amount requested (despite advice from the DFE circular to be courageous in their planning), and 15 were refused grant altogether. Priority was given to those authorities already providing a service. However, since 1990, as more authorities sought to participate in the grant system, the amount available to the DFE was spread more thinly leading to large cuts in provision for a number of authorities. Seven authorities lost more than 20% of their grants in April 1993 which led to job losses and service re-organisation. It is difficult to understand the logic behind imposing cuts on a number of successful Traveller education services, in order to finance developments of new provision elsewhere in the country, rather than providing extra resources to meet a clear need. The cuts particularly affected counties like Avon, which had submitted a bid for more grant in order to cater for the needs of a large influx of children living on Avon's already large number of unofficial camps. Government statements made it clear that it is well aware of the amount of resources required to organise appropriate education for Travellers who are forced to live a highly mobile lifestyle; the DES discussion paper quoted on p 67 highlights the unacknowledged discrimination between those on official sites and those on the roadsides. In 1993, at the time of Avon's bid for increased grant, the county, according to DoE count figures, had not only the highest number of unauthorised encampments in England, but also 48.1% of the total of unauthorised encampments in the south-west region.

Section 210 of the Education Reform Act 1988 was in many respects a major gain for Traveller children. It gave recognition and resources to the largely embryonic work that many local education authorities had been doing. However, the level of central financing in 1993/94 and consequent effects for local education authorities, appear to be negating and hampering the intentions of the ministers who framed the 1988 legislation.

Impetus from Europe

The involvement of the European organisations in Gypsy matters is not new. Following lobbying by European Gypsy organisations, the ministers of the Council of Europe adopted a succession of resolutions and recommendations from 1975 onwards urging action to reduce the marginalisation and discrimination of nomadic people and pressing governments and local authorities to improve services for Gypsies and Travellers. Intercultural education has long been on the agenda and the education issues regarding nomads have been addressed by the Council of the European Communities as well as by the Council of Europe. On 22 May 1989, ministers of education adopted EC Resolution 189/C 153/02 (no C153/3-4) 1989 on school provision for Gypsy and Traveller children, and 89/C 153/3-4 (no C153/1/2) on provision for occupational Travellers. The Resolutions and the background documents on which they are based put emphasis on the need for professionals employed in the field to share experiences and information, and a number of European conferences have been organised in different member states since 1989 with this purpose.

The 1989 Resolutions were based on the fact that there are estimated to be 1.8 million Gypsies and Travellers in the European Union (EU), over half of whom are children. There are also approximately 6 million Gypsies and Travellers elsewhere in Europe, most of them in central and eastern regions. Of the children living in the EU, only 30% to 40% of Gypsies and Travellers attend school with any regularity; half have never been to school, and only a very small percentage attend secondary school (European Union, 1994).

In June 1991, the Commission of the European Communities brought together the ministries of education of the member states for a meeting which resulted in the setting up of an ad hoc group on intercultural education, whose duties include taking an active role in the implementation of the Resolutions of 22 May 1989. In the final paragraph of the Resolutions, the Council and the ministers specified that a report should be submitted by each member state to the Council, the European Parliament and the Education Committee by the Commission before 31 December 1993. The member states have participated in compiling their reports and publication of the full set, together with a report on provision across the EU as a whole, is pending (Gypsy Research Centre, 1993).

Also in 1991, the European Parliament set up a new EU budget line to help fund work in the area of intercultural education. The ad hoc group on intercultural education, comprising representatives from national ministries of education, has two subgroups, one dealing with the children of Gypsies and Travellers and occupational Travellers, and the other with the children of migrant workers. The members of each subgroup meet three times a year to discuss the progress and possible extension of projects, proposals for the future, and common issues.

In January 1994, at a press conference carrying the title 'Quality education for everybody', the Commission of the European Communities described its proposals for a new SOCRATES programme for 1995-99, which will contribute to the development of education in all European countries. SOCRATES draws together a number of EU educational programmes in the overall framework of Articles 126/7 of the Maastricht Treaty. Action 2 of the financial provision for this work has been greatly increased from previous levels under SOCRATES. The second chapter of the SOCRATES programme is concerned with action and projects for the children of migrants and Gypsies, including occupational Travellers.

Discussion

The thrust of legislation over this century has moved full circle: from attempting to assimilate Gypsies and Travellers, the threatened removal of children from their parents (Children Act 1908); through decades of neglect, followed by legislation used to move them on tempered by a growing awareness of need brought to public consciousness by voluntary organisations; culminating in legislation framed to provide the essential funding to address those needs (Education Reform Act 1988), the top slicing of that funding and uncertainty of its future; to once again, attempting to assimilate Gypsies and Travellers through the Criminal Justice and Public Order Act 1994.

The key question for educationalists is whether the special section 210 funding will be sufficient and continue long enough for the recommendations and good practice of the HMI discussion paper 1983 and the Swann Report 1985 to be achieved. In the discussion paper, the government criticised some local education authorities in 1983, stating that: "... the responses have been insufficiently sustained to establish regular school attendance as part of the Travellers' way of life" (DES, 1983). But the abrupt change of policy on the provision of sites, if pursued in education provision, would comprise a major threat to the progress already made.

It is not possible to be optimistic on this score. We have seen that through the enactment of the Criminal Justice and Public Order Act 1994, the intention of the government of 1993/94 is to opt out, in due course, of the public provision of stopping places. The doubts which remain over specific funding for education provision for Travellers may all be part of a wider ideologically-based policy to withdraw further from services to Traveller children. This constitutes an additional pressure on Gypsy families to assimilate into the settled population if they wish to benefit from education and other statutory services. Support for this possibility can be gleaned from a comment by an HMI representative, speaking to ACERT annual general meeting in 1993, who said:

> No doubt many of us worry about the long-term future of section 210 and particularly because of changes to the character and level of section 11 funding. I think it's important that we remain optimistic about this because, after all, section 210 is enshrined within a major Education Act and was put there in response to recognised need which clearly still exists.

The same could be said of the need for more sites, but that has not inhibited the government from wishing to withdraw public provision. If we are looking for a philosophy which should underpin our commitment to the education of Traveller children, it cannot be better summed up than by a Gypsy spokesperson, MEP Juan de Dios Ramirez Heredia:

> Education, culture and knowledge in all fields are the best weapons for the effective defence of our cultural identity. As a minority, we are constantly under fire from the community at large, which has powerful means of riding roughshod over the characteristics of a people inveterately disinclined to fall

in line with the majority's cultural patterns. ... We are well aware, as Gypsies, that alone and unaided we can emerge only with difficulty from the marginal state we endure. We urgently need the help of the non-Gypsy world. ... We ask that we be consulted, and that our opinion be regarded as essential on all those questions which directly affect us. The authorities cannot simply ignore our experience, and the education departments of the various states must reckon with the Gypsies when the time comes to work out educational measures on our behalf. (Donaueschingen, 1983, 20th Council of Europe Teachers' Seminar on 'The training of teachers of Gypsy children')

Chapters 2 and 3 have comprised a discussion of the incremental development of public policy in relation to Gypsy and Traveller issues, concentrating on the processes involved at government and local authority level. We have been describing the interaction of politics and bureaucracy.

It is essentially the story of inputs and outputs of the political system, a domain jealously guarded as the preserve of politicians, administrators and professionals. What, though, of the outcomes?

The outcomes of the policy process are almost always perceived most accurately by those not involved in the shaping or influencing of original intentions. No matter how sophisticated the consultation procedures which precede modern legislation, the voices of those most directly affected are, at best, like the forlorn cry of a chorus faintly heard in the wind.

Nowhere is this more true than in the passing of laws relating to Gypsies. It is, therefore, important to examine the way these issues are received on the sites and roadsides where outcomes are what count. In the following pages we undertake two case studies dealing with the day-to-day realities of the Gypsy lifestyle. One concerns the delivery of education to travelling children, the other describes attempts to provide a basic health service to nomadic families. Both case studies are set in the county of Avon.

four

CASE STUDY I: TEACHING TRAVELLER CHILDREN IN AVON

The county of Avon is geographically the fifth smallest county in England and the ninth most densely populated and yet, according to the twice-yearly count figures published by the DoE in 1993, it has the highest number of unauthorised Traveller encampments in England (see Figure 3).

In addition to these figures, there were in 1994 a number of New Age Travellers' unauthorised encampments on 18 sites; New Age Travellers are not normally included in the DoE count figures. Avon also has 48.1% of the total unauthorised encampments in the south-west region's seven counties (see Table 5).

Table 5: **Numbers of caravans on unauthorised encampments in the south-west region of England, January 1993**

County	No.	County	No.
Avon	395	Gloucester	58
Cornwall	170	Somerset	45
Devon	53	Wiltshire	12
Dorset	88	Total	821

Source: DoE, 1993

The continuing obstacles for Travellers in gaining access to education in the years following the Caravan Sites Act 1968 varied from authority to authority. In the county of Avon, the Travellers received no educational support until 1975, three years prior to the construction in 1978 of Avon's first temporary transit site for 17 families. Lack of site provision, harassment and evictions for the majority of Travellers in the county continued to cause severe logistical problems for children's attendance at mainstream schools for the following 18 years, until Avon increased its provision to a total of two permanent and two temporary sites in 1993-94.

Figure 3: Numbers of caravans on unauthorised encampments in Avon, 1979-94

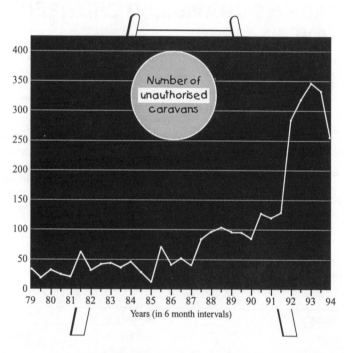

As the previous chapter has shown, the development of education provision for Travellers is so closely related to site provision that it would be difficult to present a case study of education without consideration of the myriad factors (other than school buildings and teachers) that make effective education possible. The following pages will therefore discuss how the slow development of site provision affected the lives of the Travellers to whom Avon had a duty, and how that provision influenced the rate of educational development. There were three main stages of change:

- 1975-85 with the provision of one site and a low base education service consisting of two teachers and a mobile classroom operating a segregated service;

- 1985-93 with no further site provision but the setting up of an effective county-wide education support service to Travellers;

- 1993 with the reduction of the service by 50% despite a substantial increase of numbers of Traveller children living in the county.

Figure 4: Three phases of resource allocation for the Avon education service to Traveller children

1975-85	1985-93	1993→
1 mobile classroom	2 mobile classrooms	1 head of service
2 teachers	1 head of service	4 peripatetic teachers
	1 deputy head of service	1 nursery nurse
	3 supply teachers (full-time equivalent)	1 administrative assistant
	1 administrative assistant	1 specialist education welfare officer
	6 peripatetic teachers	
	1 nursery nurse	
	2 classroom ancillaries	
	1 specialist education welfare officer	

1975-85

In 1975 Avon Local Education Authority appointed two part-time teachers as a service to meet the needs of 98 Traveller children whose families were camping unofficially in Smoke Lane, Avonmouth, north-west of the city, on land once earmarked for a site by Bristol City Council. It was expected that the two teachers, working from a van which had been converted to contain seating, would "provide preparation for school experience and initiate a vital and continuing link between school and Traveller families". The receiving schools would be in the Avonmouth area where there was some spare accommodation and it was expected that the children from the new Avonmouth site would attend school initially for two hours daily.

At the same time the new county demonstrated a positive initial response to the provision of sites, and after the decision of Bristol City Council to abandon the plans for the Smoke Lane site, the Standing Planning Consultative Committee made up of the county and district councils of Avon was asked to look in each district for land which might immediately be suitable for Gypsy caravan sites.

The county planning officer produced a commendable project brief for a 'Gypsy and other Travellers subject plan' which, it was thought, would form part of an overall structure plan for Gypsy sites. The suggested aims of the subject plan were as follows:

● to meet the requirements of the Caravan Sites Act 1968;

● to assess the present location and number, type and use made of sites and families occupying them;

● to assess the siting needs, travelling habits, living conditions and lifestyle of Gypsies and other Travellers;

● to suggest sites for securing a determined number of encampments attractive both to the Gypsies and to the general public;

● to establish standards of site provision to maintain a satisfactory level of services and facilities;

● to present recommendations that are acceptable to all interested bodies and capable of implementation by the relevant authorities.

Despite the good intentions demonstrated by these written aims, there is no record that they were acted on, other than by the provision two years later of one transit site for 17 families.

Utilising the advice in the Cripps Report, the construction of Patchway transit site provided the minimum of facilities: hard-standing, a shared cold water tap, a breeze-block toilet and large skips for waste disposal.

This was Avon's first site, destined to be its only one for 17 years, the second opening in January 1994. Travellers unsuccessful in gaining a plot on Patchway were forced to camp without water supply, elementary sanitation or refuse collection and lived under the constant threat of eviction. In addition, they were blamed for the bad conditions of these unofficial camps.

Even before the Travellers moved to Patchway site in 1978, the local schools were preparing their case against admitting Traveller children. Meetings were held to consider what action they ought to take and the authority was asked to outline its policy with regard to the admission of Travellers to school. Despite accepting that there was a statutory duty to provide education to Traveller children, the schools local to Patchway were concerned that the well-being of all children had to be considered and that children with specific needs, placed in normal classroom situations, could prove an almost impossible burden on the teacher responsible.

It was argued that there would be a real need for the provision of improved resources in staffing and capitation. The schools also voiced their apprehension regarding the antipathy of parents and the public in Patchway if one or two schools only became the focus for a large intake of Traveller children. The schools had already received statements from the settled community that their children would be transferred to other schools if Gypsy children were admitted in any number.

As a result it was agreed that although Traveller children should be fully integrated into the local education system at the earliest opportunity, it should be done with the important proviso that no school should be allowed to become a 'ghetto'. Teachers were equally concerned that adequate resources should be provided over and above the normal ratios and that staff so allocated should have the right training and experience. Various suggestions were made: that the children should receive their full-time education in a mobile school; that if they had to go to school, then it should be a school distant from Patchway so that they could first "learn acceptable behaviour"; that they "should have sufficient social graces and sufficient progress in cognitive skills before they should be allowed to go into a school near the site"; that the families should not be put under any pressure to enrol their children.

It was precisely this attitude towards Travellers that led Jean Pierre Liegeois to note some ten years later:

As long as the relations between Gypsies and Travellers and the communities which surround them remain conflictual, the relations of Gypsy/Traveller parents - and pupils with the school will remain largely determined by the negative tone of these relations, in this situation, the school has an important role to play in educating both communities towards mutual understanding and respect. (Liegeois, 1986)

As it happened, the local opposition and harassment previously mentioned was so intense when the site officially opened in 1978, that the Travellers were totally resistant to the idea of formal education other than on-site provision where they would be assured of their children's safety. For the following decade, the van made daily visits to the site, teaching children six at a time, in approximately one hour sessions. Despite the original aim to work on site using mobile provision as a 'bridge' to getting the children to schools, the local hostility had led to such intense mutual mistrust between the local schools and the Travellers that it proved to be too great an obstacle to school attendance.

Prior to the official opening of Patchway site, the two part-time teachers attempted to address the needs of both the Patchway children, then still unofficially encamped, and nearly 70 other highly mobile clients who were constantly under the threat of eviction from three unofficial sites in other parts of the county. It was a token service. The needs were immense.

An early review

In a review of the service in 1976, the education officer who was responsible for the education of Travellers, wrote in his report that the primary aims of the service when it was set up in 1975 bore little relationship to the apparent needs of the children, and that "it should be regarded as the first step in the educational process of this deprived group". Table 6 illustrates the age range and numbers of children receiving on-site support at the time of the review.

Progress of the 50 pupils contacted was monitored by the teachers over the period of one year when they recorded that 25 children had shown "improvement in their social skills", 11 children had "improved in both social and learning skills" and 10 children were "ready for some school experience". This confirmed the teachers' impressions that there were two distinct groups forming with different needs, one which could be introduced to school, and one which would need a further 'bridging' period.

Table 6: **School-aged children on four sites serviced by the mobile classroom in Avon, 1975**

	Rising 5s	Primary	Secondary	Total
No. children on site	15	34	19	68*
No. children contacted	14	26	10	50†

Notes: * The teachers were aware of a further 30 children from other unofficial sites but were unable to make contact due to insufficient time
     † The discrepancy between children on site and children contacted was due to;
        a) boys over 11 years helping their fathers with their work
        b) the two half-time teachers' shortage of time to make contact with all the children on site

Source: Avon County Council

In February 1977, following the review of the service, Avon's chief education officer submitted a report to the education sub-committee on the Traveller education service, with a recommendation that it should be improved to provide a county-wide service. The two half-time teachers had been making regular visits to four sites in Avon, although it was known that there were other sites used by Travellers whose children had no contact with the education service at all.

The education sub-committee agreed to appoint the two half-time teachers to full-time posts and to provide a fully equipped mobile classroom to replace the van. The cost of the teachers' salaries was reimbursed under the 'no-area' pooling arrangements. There were further recommendations from the education department to the education committee to increase the teaching staff to four and provide another mobile classroom to work with children from an additional large encampment on the south side of the city, but this was not achieved. The committee requested "to be kept informed on the needs of the Traveller education service as appropriate". There were, however, no further reports to committee until ten years later. For many involved in the debate and in meeting children's needs, the hidden agenda appeared to be 'no authorised site - no extended educational provision'.

In the following decade, the 'mobile school', a converted Ford Transit, provided segregated education for approximately 100

Traveller children in Avon. The teachers were attached to the multi-cultural education centre and given clear guidelines: they should first establish contact with Travellers and their children; enhance the social competence of each child; improve cognitive skills; give limited school experience in order to prepare for acceptance of school and acceptance in school; and transfer pupils to normal full-time education when they were likely to succeed. The failure of the latter two guidelines was inevitable given the lack of permanent sites, the constant evictions, the reluctance of the schools and insufficient time or resources for the teachers to deal with the issues of prejudice and discrimination both in schools and in relation to sites.

At that time, there were three distinct groups of Travellers resorting to Avon. The county identified them as showmen, Romanies and Tinkers (now referred to as showmen, English and Welsh Gypsies and Irish and Scottish Travellers). Very little support was offered to the showmen's children because the authority felt that the parents were generally financially secure and received adequate advice on education through the Showmen's Guild. When significant numbers of fairground children were admitted to schools for the winter season, extra staff or capitation was temporarily provided to the school by the authority.

The majority of Travellers living on the only county site at Patchway were English and Welsh Gypsies and the mobile school visited every morning, teaching six children at a time in one hour sessions. Thus each child on site received five hours tuition weekly with the ratio 3:1.

The Irish Travellers, who were mostly forced to live on the unofficial stopping places in Avon, only received visits from the mobile school during one afternoon per week, and only then when they camped in small numbers. This was because of the impossibility of working on some encampments which could be home to 100 or more children of school age.

There was also at that time a small group of New Age Travellers, known locally as Rainbow Warriors, residing in the county who were also excluded from mobile provision because of insufficient time, but the teachers visited their camp once a fortnight for one hour to provide the children with a limited distance-learning-programme which was overseen by the parents who were mostly literate and therefore able to help their children to develop literacy and numeracy skills.

It should also be stressed that some English and Welsh Gypsies had been settled in Avon for many years and their children were relatively accustomed to attending local primary schools. Regular secondary attendance created more of a problem, mainly because of the early adult status of Gypsy youth, and also because of parents' fear that their children would learn different codes of behaviour related to, for example, sex or drugs.

By 1979 the numbers of Travellers residing in Avon began to rise steadily as neighbouring counties achieved 'designation' status. Official figures indicated that the number of unofficial encampments in Avon had almost trebled between 1979 and 1988 (Figure 3). Conditions on these sites were appalling and evictions could happen within days of each other. As evictions took place, so the land would be mounded or 'ditched out' to prevent return. The systematic barring of stopping places meant the systematic denial of basic services to Travellers. The lack of running water or refuse collection; the difficulty in obtaining, and sometimes the refusal of health care; harassment, often taking the form of physical attack; the lack of social support; and above all the often derelict, always dangerous, surroundings in which they were forced to live - all contributed to an understandable lack of school uptake.

Despite the well intended aims of the 'Gypsy and Travellers subject plan', written in 1975 by an enlightened county planning officer, in one decade Avon had achieved only one transit site with minimal amenities. Many education officers were fully committed to providing educational opportunities for the children but the local education authority did not significantly improve its segregated token education service until ten years later.

However, despite the fact that there was no marked change in permanent site provision until 1993, the educational provision gradually improved until, during the years 1987-93, Avon Local Education Authority developed one of the most effective Traveller education support services in the country. From unpromising beginnings, the collaboration between voluntary agencies, teachers and Gypsies themselves, began to provide what became a nationally recognised model of good practice.

1985-92

The improvement to Avon's low base educational provision was influenced mainly by national developments already described in

Chapter 3, but local developments also greatly contributed to the gradual increase in awareness, not only of the educational needs of Travellers, but also of their cultures and lifestyles. The three factors which most influenced county decisions were the substantial increase in numbers of Traveller children living on unauthorised encampments, who were unable to gain access to schools given the limited time that the two mobile school teachers could spend in the south side of the city; the commitment of education officers, head teachers and the mobile school teachers; and the continuous exchange of information during 1985 and 1986 between ACERT, Avon Traveller Support Group and the county council.

Following the publication of the Swann Report in 1985, the director of education wrote to all schools in Avon, reminding them of their duty to Traveller children.   Shortly after this, the two specialist teachers were unexpectedly able to work with Travellers on the encampments south of the city because the mobile classroom was undergoing major repair and testing. They took the opportunity to spend the time assisting Traveller parents with the placement of 25 children into five schools, three primary and two secondary. The schools were anxious to help and the Travellers' teachers gave as much information and advice as the limited time allowed.

They were unable to give in-class support due to the large number of children involved and the limited time before they were due to return to their full teaching programme in the mobile classroom. Six weeks later, they discovered that not one of the 25 children had remained in any of the five schools. Following consultation with each school and the families, the teachers recorded in their termly report that although the reasons for the failure of the placements were complex, it was clear that lack of in-school support following the enrolments and the constant evictions, making daily life on sites extremely difficult for families, were the major causes of the non-attendance.

A letter was sent to the director of education, informing him of the situation and asking for his help. His response was to request the advisor for multi-cultural education and the education officer with responsibility for equal opportunities, to prepare a report to committee on the education of Traveller children. He added:

> It is anticipated that the report will evaluate current provision against perceived shortfall together with the recommendations of the Swann Report. In that context, the observations which you have made, both in writing and verbally, together with

information from the Travellers' children unit, is proving of great assistance. (Avon County Council, 1985)

But there were no further developments, despite pressure from schools, until eight months later when a particular incident became the catalyst for further progress. The head teacher of one of the five schools involved in the attempted placements of Traveller children earlier that year, tried to reinstate five children who had been enrolled previously. They had moved from the unauthorised site to a council house which they had 'taken over' from previous tenants; an eviction order had been served with a court hearing pending. The children, aged from five to eleven, had no previous school experience and were first generation school attenders.

All efforts were made by the school staff to settle the children, and the mobile classroom teachers assisted during the first three mornings, but following the withdrawal of this specialised help, the situation deteriorated and resulted in the head teacher's reluctant exclusion of the youngest child whose behaviour became uncontrollable. The older siblings had settled well but the head teacher admitted feeling ill-prepared to deal with their needs, there being no expertise within the staff to provide a meaningful learning environment for the children, who had no previous school experience, were non-literate, and were from the travelling community. The three mornings' support from the mobile school staff was successful but insufficient. Other head teachers in the same circumstances shared this concern.

The school educational psychologist was asked to assess the children and reported that they did not have special educational needs, which could have led to 'statementing', thus qualifying them for additional teaching support within the school. She agreed with the mobile school teacher, however, that the children did have specific needs for which there was no policy of support by the local education authority. She was, therefore, unable to recommend a course of action which would answer the complex needs of the children.

However, she called a meeting to discuss the issue bringing together senior education officers, the principal educational psychologist, the education officer for special education, the assistant education officer for staffing, the head of the multi-cultural education centre, the head of the school and the mobile school teachers. After discussing the nature of appropriate provision for two and a half hours, the options available looked limited:

- mobile school - ideal, but cannot be spared from its normal time-table in Northavon;

- supply teacher - possible but problematic because of lack of space and resources needed (medical room at school?);

- full-time 'floating' teacher attached to multi-cultural education centre - problematic because of funding;

- full-time teacher attached to mobile school - good, but would have to go to committee;

- home-tutor system - possible because flexible.

Finally, it was decided in the short term that home tuition would be provided temporarily for the youngest child for one hour daily until the outcome of the eviction order was known and the situation reviewed. The home-tutor would be working in very difficult circumstances, with no heating in the house and no access to usual school resources. The child would need access to a wealth of education play material that neither his home nor a medical room was going to provide. The other four children would receive the support of a half-time teacher until the point of their full integration.

In their conclusions, the officers recommended:

- that the situation should be reviewed when the family were rehoused;

- that there should be a procedure for heads of schools when enrolling children from the travelling community who have no previous school experience or are older non-literate children (it should be noted that this is not the case with all Traveller children);

- that problems with staffing and funding should be resolved;

- that the problem of 'place' with resource material should be resolved;

- that the amount of mobile school capitation should be reviewed if the mobile school is to provide resource material for home tuition;

- that in-service training should be arranged to heighten teachers' awareness of the needs of the children from travelling communities;

• that the assistant education officer (staffing) and the education officer (special education) should liaise with the advisor for multi-cultural education and the education officer with responsibility for equal opportunities who are reviewing the Traveller education service in Avon.

(Avon County Council, 1985b)

The long-term consequence of this incident proved to be of vital importance to the development of Traveller education in the county, in that by agreeing to liaise with the officers identified by the director of education as those involved with the review of the Traveller education service, the officers who participated in the meeting were instrumental not only in pressing the urgency of the issue but also in being able to bring a 'real' school situation to the debate.   The circumstances of the meeting, where the ethos was caring and supportive, were also valuable in terms of relationships.

The school remained welcoming to Traveller children and had further developed its links with the mobile school teachers, as well as feeling valued and supported by the authority.   The education officers, in executing their duty, had also participated in an awareness raising exercise, of a community about whom they admitted to knowing very little.   The mobile school teachers had made contact with lead officers who, although they were not aware of it at the time, were destined to support them for many years to come.

In the following month, December 1985, one of the mobile school teachers was asked to prepare a report to inform a meeting which had been set up by the authority to review the structure of the multi-cultural education centre.   (The Traveller education service had been 'tagged on' to the centre during the late 1970s in an attempt to reduce the isolation of the two teachers.)

In preparation, the mobile school teachers counted the number of Traveller children on unauthorised encampments who were not attending school and who, with the limited time available, they were not able to reach with the mobile school.   They counted 270 children not receiving any education and 27 receiving two hours a week mobile provision from sites in the city and to the south.   At that time, the mobile school was still operating mainly in the north of the city with 40 children from the one authorised site and three private sites. These children received approximately one hour a day tuition.

The numbers of children not attending mainstream school thus totalled 337. In consultation with the parents of the children counted, the teachers were astounded by the number of Travellers who were not aware that their children actually had the right to attend school. The majority of the unofficially camped Travellers at that time were Irish, many of them newcomers to Avon. Some families had assumed, having been turned away from schools so often, that the main obstacle was because they were 'foreign', and for that reason were not entitled to education while out of their country of origin.

Others were well aware of carrying the double load of anti-Irish and anti-Traveller discrimination. What they all shared was a keenness to send their children to school, reinforced by, rather than in spite of, the appalling conditions of the encampments on which they were forced to live.

The report, which included names, ages and location of the Traveller children, was presented to the authority in March 1986. Those at the multi-cultural education centre restructuring meeting needed no further evidence of need. After reading the teacher's short report, which had been circulated to them at the meeting, the chair of the meeting commented, "I think we are not saying anything because we are so deeply shocked and ashamed that we don't really know what to say. How could 337 school-aged children slip through the net in our authority?".

By way of immediate response a full-time teacher on a fixed-term contract was appointed to the mobile school in order to release one of its two teachers to begin work in south Bristol unauthorised sites, introducing the children to mainstream schools.

However, the task of the single-handed teacher to find school placements for such a large number of children was not easy. In her summer term report 1986, she wrote:

The parents of the 270 Traveller children identified earlier this year as not receiving any form of education, have moved around the south side of the city following numerous evictions, making mainstream school attendance impossible to arrange and maintain without transport facilities. During the past three weeks, I have stopped visiting two of the sites as I feel we have nothing to offer. Parents who were hopeful regarding school enrolment for their children six months ago, when we conducted the survey, are now becoming disenchanted. Some are very angry. We desperately need school transport so that the children maintain attendance at the original school of enrolment despite the constant evictions, which are in themselves traumatic enough.

One year later, in September 1987, the restructuring of the service finally took place, funded by the 'no-area pool'. The title Mobile School was changed to Avon Traveller Education Group (ATEG), and the service remained temporarily under the 'umbrella' of the multi-cultural education centre. In 1987 ATEG consisted of:

- a coordinator
- 7 peripatetic support teachers
- a full-time clerical assistant
- 600 days of supply teacher support
- an office and resource base
- 2 mobile classrooms

By 1990 an education welfare officer, a nursery nurse, extra supply teacher hours and classroom assistant hours had been added to the service. One of the two mobile classrooms was removed from the service. The stated aims of the group were:

- to help facilitate the successful integration of Traveller children into mainstream schooling;

- to assist the class teacher to meet the education and social needs of Traveller children;

- to develop and provide resource material to encourage a positive self-image in Traveller children and also to support a more positive understanding of Travellers' lifestyle among other children;

- to assist in forming links between home and school;

- to help the class teacher to assess the children and identify special educational needs if they exist (and help the teacher to differentiate between the specific needs that arise as a result of intermittent schooling and special educational needs);

- to advise all school staff on matters of Travellers' lifestyle and culture;

- to support the children and the school in effectively tackling anti-Traveller racism when it occurs.

After a short period of training, the newly appointed teachers were placed in schools identified to receive an intake of children from the unauthorised sites. However, much of the coordinator's time was taken up in health and welfare issues among Traveller children. Only approximately 5% of Travellers had access to pitches on county sites and, therefore, most were subject to the hazardous and unhealthy conditions prevailing on unauthorised sites, and to evictions.

ATEG felt it was important to give active attention not only to the issues which affected Travellers on site but also to the problems which undermined the efforts to make the school experience meaningful. This created an additional workload which was outside the role and experience of the coordinator who tried to fulfil a multiplicity of roles such as site provision advocate, health visitor and education welfare officer.

Another difficulty was maintaining the school attendance of children following evictions. Without special transport facilities, it was not possible to maintain attendance at the original schools if Travellers were forced to move outside the radius which entitled them to school transport under the terms of the local education authority's transport policy. Despite a steady flow of successful enrolments, the success rate of full integration was hampered by the lack of continuity in attendance.

In March 1988, seven months after the restructuring of the Traveller education service, the local education authority appointed a full-time specialist education welfare officer for Traveller children attached to, and physically based with, the new team of teachers.

In the same year, the local education authority created a new education officer post with responsibility for equal opportunities. Part of this officer's duty was the oversight of ATEG, now an autonomous unit. In the autumn of 1988 two important documents were approved by the authority: a policy statement on the education of Travellers and a transport policy, which ensured that transport would be made available for Traveller children, if required, following evictions.

At county level, ATEG was represented on a multi-agency Traveller services group which coordinated information and matters affecting Travellers, and passed on recommendations to elected members of the county council. The services group initiated a programme of training for key workers in the council. ATEG implemented this with social services, the education welfare service and community leisure personnel as a multi-agency venture. In 1989 the county appointed a full-time Traveller liaison officer, and in 1990 the health authority appointed a specialist health visitor for Travellers.

In April 1990, the 'no-area pool' funding was replaced by a specific grant which came into effect in April 1990 under section 210 of the Education Reform Act 1988. Funding was allocated to Avon from the DFE after the submission of a successful bid, to improve levels of enrolment and attendance and to facilitate Traveller children's access to the national curriculum. In contrast to 'no-area pool' funding when claims were made retrospectively, bids have to be made in advance, supported by detailed plans. The grant normally provides 75% funding for the service during a period of three years. The education policy for Travellers approved by Avon education committee in 1989 formed the backcloth for the bid.

During the following three years, the county continued to improve the service to Travellers by appointing a nursery nurse, temporary classroom assistants and school lunch-time assistants until 1993 when they had almost matched the funding received through the DFE grant. At its peak the ATEG structure was one of the support services to schools, fully integrated into the county structure.

The effectiveness of ATEG was monitored through successful enrolments, continued attendance and educational progress reports, as required by the terms of the specific grant funding. Informally effectiveness was measured by continuous consultation with Traveller children and their parents.

The aims of ATEG, in relation to access to and benefit from mainstream education and improved relationships between schools and Travellers had been achieved but needed to be maintained, especially in the face of continuing lack of site provision in Avon and increasing numbers of Traveller children in the county.

Figure 5: Structure of Avon Traveller Education Group

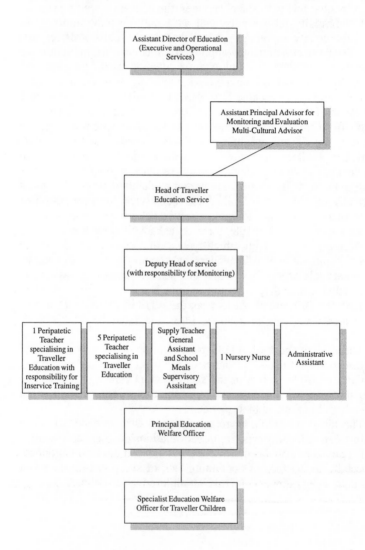

1993

Consequently, a second three-year project bid was submitted to the DFE for 1993-96, which reflected the cost of the improved existing service and an additional amount to aid the cost of providing for the increased number of children on unauthorised encampments. However, the bid was not accepted and, furthermore, the amount of direct grant aid awarded reflected a 15% reduction on the previous year's grant amount.

Avon education committee was not able to make up the shortfall because of the financial situation facing the council which needed to cut its education budget by £5,438 million in order to meet government targets. The existing education service to Travellers was reduced by 50% at a time when the number of children needing support had increased from 201 at the start of the first three-year project in 1990 to 299 at the time of the second project bid in October 1992. Staff cuts to the service were as follows:

- three full-time specialist teachers;

- supply teacher hours equivalent to three full-time posts;

- general assistant hours equivalent to two full-time posts;

- reduced staff travel (between schools and sites and schools);

- the mobile nursery classroom;

- a large reduction in transport for pupils from sites to schools;

- a large reduction in books, equipment and clothing grants.

This scale of reduction meant that the activities of ATEG had to be reviewed from 1 April 1993. Within days, the implementation of the reduced transport resources for Traveller children affected 15 families who had been evicted, causing a major upheaval as new schools, transport arrangements, support teacher placements and school record transfer had to be re-organised. The revised arrangements for transport also meant that children were being enrolled at the school nearest to a site, thus increasing numbers in those schools dramatically. Large numbers of children needing support in one school can create a situation which may not be in the children's best interest or the school's, given the reduced number of ATEG staff.

In-class support, nationally recognised as good practice for Traveller children with limited school experience, was also discontinued. ATEG was no longer able to operate its policy of supporting schools in providing pupils with full access to the classroom curriculum.

Meanwhile, under pressure from ministers, the county council had committed itself from October 1989 to providing sites, and decided in the meanwhile not always to evict Travellers from its own land. The secretary of state issued a direction under the provisions of section 9 of the Caravan Sites Act 1968 on 31 October 1990, requiring Avon to provide accommodation for a further 80 caravans. In February 1992, at a major Travellers sub-committee meeting, councillors discussed the urgent need to provide permanent Traveller sites within Avon. A large number of resolutions were passed including the acceptance of the need to provide 100 additional pitches in the county, either by local authority or private provision, while recognising this figure would need to be reviewed as more information on the level and type of need was obtained. Despite the urgent need, it was not until two years later in February 1994, that the county's first permanent site was opened.

For the first time, the local education authority's reduced education support service was able to assist parents living on a permanent site to choose schools for their children on a parity with the rest of the community, under the terms of the Education Act 1944.

It had taken Avon 24 years to begin to comply with the Caravan Sites Act 1968, during which time ATEG had developed from a token resource to an effective county-wide service, and been reduced once again to a low base resource with its funding halved. The cuts happened as a positive trend of Traveller parent involvement in educational choices was developing and when the number of Traveller children in need of support had increased substantially.

It is possible to illustrate a direct relationship between national policy and local effect (Figure 6). The decisions taken in Whitehall had an impact on local authority budgets, having in the case of Gypsy children an immediate and detrimental effect on the lives of families living on both authorised and unauthorised sites. Figure 6 demonstrates the annual growth in the number of children receiving teacher, general assistant or nursery nurse support in primary and secondary schools in Avon between 1982 and 1993. The figures are

These are the Gypsy children of Avon pictured in their mobile schools. For the most part, they were born and brought up on the roadside verges and unofficial encampments which spread across the county. In 1979 there were between 20 and 30 caravans noted in the area but by 1993 the number had increased to 390. No-one has ever assessed the total child population arising from these homes.

Photos: Nathalie Beaufils © ATEG

In 1975 about 50 children were in contact with segregated formal education activities; by the early 1980s there were over 70, mainly of primary school age, receiving teaching for up to two hours a week. But then in 1985 a local survey recorded over 270 children receiving no education at all. However, with the expansion of Avon's Traveller Education Group, progress was rapid and by 1992 over 320 children were receiving support in full-time education.

Reports from a specialist health visitor working with travelling families in the early 1990s recorded over 37% of unofficial sites having no water or sanitation and no regular refuse collection. The families faced considerable difficulty in obtaining access to health care, antenatal services and GP registration. High levels of accidental injury in the home include cuts, burns and falls. These children are more prone to illness such as impetigo, dysentery and respiratory infection than their counterparts in the settled population.

A campaign in Bristol to improve welfare benefit take-up among Gypsies and Travellers demonstrated a 60% increase in take-up during the campaign period, with Child Benefit applications increasing more than any other. Avon's travelling children are just some of the 19,000 estimated to live in England and Wales, more than a third of whom have no legal site on which their parents can stop without fear of prosecution and intimidation.

a 'snap-shot' count on a particular day each year and do not attempt to assess the total number of children who may have attended occasionally, or who had received support but no longer needed it, or did not need support from the outset. However, the figure indicates quite clearly how changes of county policy affected the enrolment and attendance of Traveller children over time.

Figure 6:   Trends in children receiving teacher support by ATEG, 1982-93

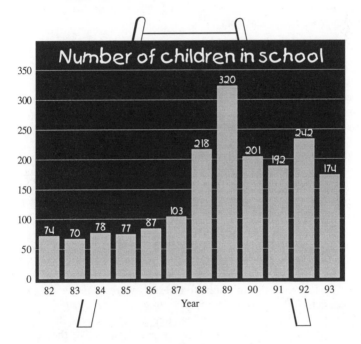

Between 1982 and 1984, the only resource was a mobile classroom staffed by two teachers. Approximately half the children contacted received one hour's teaching a day, and the other half, two hours a week. Included in the figures for the same year are small numbers of fairground children who were enrolled in schools during winter. Schools received a small increase in staffing during the period of their stay.

Figure 6 illustrates that from 1985 to 1986, when additional supply teachers were allocated to schools enrolling Traveller children who had no previous school experience, the numbers increased slightly. From September 1987, following the formation of ATEG, numbers increased significantly as children were enrolled full-time in schools and offered in-class support.

The reduction of financial support by 50% in March 1993 caused a 50% cut in ATEG teaching staff and a consequent drop in the numbers of children supported by the group and the amount of support available for each child, clearly illustrated in Figure 6. The figures for 1993 also represent a change in the type of support, from full in-class support to small group withdrawal in the area of language development only.

Conclusion

The development of education policy and provision described in this chapter applies only to Avon; service structures have varied in other authorities, but the overall story is similar in many areas, illustrating nationally the weakness of the 1968 legislation. By dealing with the provision of sites in isolation from other vital services, it encouraged a lack of coordination between departments at local level where, despite apparent corporate approaches to Traveller issues, with joint committees and inter-agency cooperation, service delivery remained limited, ad hoc and prone to disruption.

At its peak, the education service for Traveller children in Avon was, by most standards, good and many local officers gave their professional support, despite the prejudice or lack of political will at member level. But whilst positive results were achieved in regard to access to, and the benefits of, schooling, the lack of site provision resulted in exclusion and disadvantage. The irony is that by the time more sites were provided by the county in 1994, the funding for the education service had already been cut.

This case study demonstrates that we still have some way to go if we are to meet the reasonable demands articulated by one Gypsy spokesman at an educational conference:

> There is no other community in the United Kingdom that is persecuted from the cradle to the grave for simply trying to live the life that Gypsy people have lived for centuries. ... We demand the right to a proper education for all Gypsy people - the right to bring up our children in our own way without fear

of persecution or intimidation, and to be treated on an equal basis with everybody else: no more, and definitely no less. (Mercer, 1992)

five

CASE STUDY II:
HEALTH CARE IN AVON - THE
TRAVELLER EXPERIENCE

The county of Avon has perhaps the greatest concentration of Gypsies and Travellers of any part of the United Kingdom and in 1989 a jointly-funded proposal to set up a dedicated service for itinerants was agreed by health care providers in the county. In May 1990 a specialist health visitor (SHV) was appointed, with the principal aim of improving the health of travelling women and children, and improving their access to health care generally.

This case study draws on the work of the SHV between May 1990 and November 1992 and utilises unpublished statistics and reports of her activities (UBHT, 1993). Some comparisons are made with similar studies in Kent in 1986 (Pahl and Vaile, 1988).

At the time of the study, the population of Travellers in the county was about 219 caravans not including New Age Travellers, based upon the twice-yearly counts published by the DoE. However, in practice, the population was in constant flux and was boosted at key times by attendance at such occasions as the Glastonbury festival, the Stow fair and major music events.

Observations by the SHV during this period suggest she was serving 29 sites in Avon, 26 of which were unauthorised encampments, and five of which were privately-owned. New Age groups resided in 12 of these sites, with English and Welsh Gypsies in five and Irish Travellers in eight.

At peak summer months, over 700 children under 16 years were counted in the area. In November 1992, the SHV had over 120 families on her caseload (see Table 7). Over the two and a half years covered by her report she was in face-to-face contact with 536 families in total.

The complex geographical and institutional context of the project was further complicated by health service reforms which were implemented during the period and make accurate statistical analysis difficult. The 'purchaser' agency is the Bristol and District Health Authority with the 'provider' being a newly created United Bristol Health Care Trust (UBHT) made up of four previous health districts. The area spanned by the work of the SHV includes the county of Avon, six district councils and four health districts. Table 7 shows the distribution of travelling families over this administrative area.

Table 7: **Site location and population by health district in Avon, November 1992**

Health district	No. of families	Under 5s	Over 5s
UBHT	11	9	18
Frenchay	54	51	54
Southmead	52	39	77
Weston*	10	?3	?8

Note: * The Weston site was not visited by SHV after August 1992.

Typically, during the period of study, the spread of children between various groups of Travellers is shown in Table 8, with a preponderance of over-5s except among New Age groups, who were markedly younger parents themselves and had no generational history of nomadism.

Table 8: **Population of Traveller children by type in Avon, November 1992**

Type	Under 5s	Over 5s
Irish Travellers	47	73
New Age	34	20+
Gypsy/English Travellers	21	54+

Because of the failure of the county council and local district councils to agree on official sites, the county is under a directive from the secretary of state to provide at least 100 individual pitches. At the time of the case study it had 34 temporary pitches, all with basic amenities. However, the county has also tolerated illegal occupancy of its own land, much of which is wasteland, demolition sites or redundant highway close to main roads.

The SHV reported consistently on the 'appalling' condition of these and other unauthorised encampments; 37% lacking basic facilities such as water and sanitation, in some cases water having to be fetched from long distances and having to be paid for. On these sites, domestic refuse is not regularly collected and "can become rat-infested within days".

Factors influencing the health of Travellers

At the start of the special project, it was evident that four main factors were important in the failure of basic health care reaching travelling families. These were identified by the SHV as:

- evident hostility and unwelcoming behaviour by receptionists and members of the public at surgeries, dental waiting rooms and clinics, resulting in humiliation and rejection;

- lack of information about services, due partly to illiteracy and also to the lack of a postal address for health education material;

- culturally-based lack of recognition by Travellers of precise dates, times, ages etc and of clocks, telephones and other modern devices which allow the bureaucracy of an over-used health service to function, but which make no allowances for minority cultures unfamiliar with highly-programmed procedures;

- difficulties in registering family members with a general practitioner and, because of 'no fixed abode', problems of registering for any form of primary health care service.

Anecdotally, it was in most cases said to be the hostility of receptionists which presented the main barrier.

Illness and environmental conditions

Preliminary observations by the SHV suggested that the environmental circumstances of Travellers made them particularly vulnerable to respiratory illness, enteric infections such as dysentery, skin disorders such as impetigo, and infections like hepatitis 'A' and 'B'. Poor sanitation, lack of a pure water supply and a low level of awareness of cleanliness by some groups, were at the root of these phenomena.

A high level of accidental injury on sites was also noted in the preliminary investigations of the SHV. Cuts from broken glass and metal, accidental poisoning by ingestion of diesel and other liquids, exposure to open sewage, or from chemicals for use in portable toilets, were recorded.

Confined space within caravans has resulted in a higher than normal level of burns, scalds and falls among younger children, although this was noticeably more prevalent among New Age groups, with less familiarity of caravan habitation and less conventional types of vehicle being used for domestic activity.

The proximity of major roads was identified as a danger to children; one fatality was recorded during the period covered by the SHV's report; exposure to such dangers was identified as a direct consequence of failure to provide officially designed sites.

Welfare rights

At the beginning of the study period the SHV noted a considerable lack of take-up of welfare benefits and took active steps to improve levels. Among the major reasons identified were the inability to give fixed postal addresses and lack of literacy or ability to cope with form-filling.

Measures taken during the study period included the recruitment of colleagues in other agencies to enquire about receipt of benefits, accompanying families to appropriate offices and the involvement of welfare rights officers from Bristol City Council in a targeted campaign of benefit take-up.

During the period of the study it is estimated that there was more than 60% increase in the number of families receiving some level of benefit, although the high level of mobility, especially at seasons of music festival activity, make this difficult to quantify. There was also a reduction in the level of street begging by New Age groups, directly consequent upon the regular receipt of family income supplement.

Access to health care

The case study, based upon the work of the SHV between May 1990 and November 1992, and against the background of political and social conflict over facilities for travelling families in Avon, does not attempt to make distinctions between one kind of travelling group and another, except where these highlight differing factors in analysing health care.

Whilst the county and district councils were struggling with definitions and categorisation enshrined in the 1968 Act, as part of the site provision programme, the health providers and the SHV made no such distinctions, and attempted to improve the service to all nomadic people. Regular visits to all sites were used to collect routine health information in a semi-structured interview.

It is clear that general practitioners (GPs) have generally treated Travellers as temporary residents and 70% of the SHV caseload received that level of care and advice. However, 10% are registered permanently with one practice, using a central address for correspondence, but are frequently living over two miles from their surgery. The remaining 20% expect to use accident and emergency departments of local hospitals throughout Avon.

Based upon structured interviews with each family, the study showed that 80% of all Travellers had been refused treatment at one time or another whilst in the Avon area.

Maternal health

Travelling women tend to marry at young ages and 16 years is not uncommon. They have larger than average families and the study in Avon found that six children was the average and ten not uncommon.

Access to antenatal care can be difficult, especially for families who move frequently or travel extensively. The introduction by the SHV of hand-held (as opposed to computer-based) antenatal records made significant improvements in continuity of care.

At the beginning of the project, referral to antenatal clinic was via the GP service, but difficulties of registration meant, in some cases, a six week delay before the client was seen in an antenatal clinic. Once the SHV was able to negotiate that she could make direct referrals, some 82 mothers were seen at clinics in the Avon area during the project period.

Of these, 38 delivered in the maternity units within Avon and 3 more had home confinements; the remainder continued to travel and no record of their delivery exists. The outcome of these cases is unknown. Of the three home confinements, one was born with no medical attendance sought, either in the antenatal or labour period.

These statistics may be compared with other studies carried out among travelling families in Kent and Sheffield, where it was found that prenatal mortality rates were higher among travelling families. In Sheffield, for example, a cluster of six prenatal deaths out of twelve births to Traveller women were noted between January and August 1982 (Peck, 1983).

In Kent, in a study by Pahl and Vaile, 263 travelling women were interviewed (see Table 9). It was found here that still-birth and infant mortality rates were higher for mothers on private sites and unauthorised sites than on local authority sites. This suggests a correlation with higher levels of mobility (Pahl and Vaile, 1988). Table 9 compares the Kent figures with national infant mortality rates.

Table 9:   Comparison of mortality rates in the Kent study and national rates

Mortality rates (per 1,000 live births)	Kent study	National rates
Prenatal mortality	16	9
Still-birth	12	7
Infant mortality	17.5	11

The figures for Avon are those recorded during the period of the project, but because of the small sample cannot be compared with national figures. They show that between May 1990 and November 1992 there were 41 live births given by Traveller women in the Avon area. No stillbirths are recorded and no infant deaths occurred. One small child was killed following a 'hit and run' incident whilst the family were camped at the side of a busy road.

Birth control

Some Traveller women tend to have large families more as a result of family and partner pressure than because of a preference of their own. However, the Avon survey indicated that many women have changed their attitudes in recent years. Information gleaned from in-depth interviews by the SHV as part of health screening work, suggests that physical exhaustion following repeated pregnancies and financial hardship are the main reasons for spacing families. Interviews indicate that this often entails using contraceptive methods without the husband's knowledge, to limit the possibility of pregnancy.

Limited literacy makes it difficult to consider prescribing the pill and the study revealed that some women take pills at random. Anecdotal evidence suggests that as a result of poor literacy, many women lack knowledge of basic female and male anatomy and therefore the choice of contraception among Travellers varies: the SHV interviews demonstrated that the most common methods used are the IUCD and injectable methods (see Table 10).

Table 10: Preferred contraceptive methods among Traveller women in Avon

Contraception methods	% of women
I.U.C.D.	60
Injectable methods	20
Pill	3
Barrier methods	10
Unknown/not using	7

Ruston (1990) believes that for those Travellers who are practising Catholics, only the rhythm method is acceptable, but the SHV in Avon reported that among large numbers of Catholic Irish women, their decision was not governed by religion, but the choice of method most suitable for their needs.

Child health

In the culture of traditional Gypsy and Traveller groups child care has a high priority, but there still maintain relatively high levels of childhood morbidity, mainly because of poor environmental conditions and the difficulties of access to health care.

Of the 41 births to these groups in Avon during the project period, 3 did not receive a primary visit from health visitors; of these, one refused the health visiting service and the other two had moved on before the primary visit was due. One baby was born prematurely at 32 weeks; the remainder were born between 37 and 41 weeks.

From other studies and published accounts of Traveller child health referred to above, there is evidence of an increasing prevalence of low birth weight. However, in Avon, one baby was classified as small, for dates, but the average weight of those born during the study was 3.48kg, which is comparable to the average of the settled population.

The study supported the view that breast-feeding among traditional groups is very rare, although very common in earlier generations and as recently as 20 years ago. Women said that changes in clothing and fashion meant that the privacy afforded by the traditional shawl, no longer available, is a cause of this change. Lack of privacy was the main reason offered by both Gypsies and Irish Travellers for not breast-feeding.

However, all babies born to New Age Traveller mothers were breast-fed and this was continued after the introduction of solids, usually at 4-5 months. Mothers in traditional groups introduced solids often as early as 10 days, but the average introduction was at 8 weeks.

The Kent study (Pahl and Vaile, 1988) observed that there was a low take-up of immunisation among Traveller children, and to increase the take-up in Avon the SHV introduced a new domiciliary immunisation service. This commenced in Bristol district in November 1990 and was extended to Frenchay district in February 1991, and to Southmead district in November 1991.

Some confusion ensued among the Travellers, for whom health district boundaries have little meaning, but during the project period, with the exception of three families, the whole child population among travelling families who had direct contact with the SHV were successfully immunised (see Table 11).

The SHV reports that practice and predilection vary between Traveller groups with regard to the efficacy of immunisation. English Travellers tend to want protection against diphtheria, tetanus and polio, but refuse pertussis and the measles, mumps and rubella vaccine. This can cause difficulties for GPs whose targets are affected if large numbers of Gypsies reside in their area.

Table 11: **Immunisation given to Traveller children in Avon, May 1990 to November 1992**

Immunisations	
DT and Polio	134
DPT and Polio	62
Measles, Mumps and Rubella (MMR)	33
Pre-school booster	24
Rubella	4
Hib vaccine	5
Total	262

Pahl and Vaile (1988) point out that epidemics of infectious disease have not been reported among travelling Gypsies, despite the low immunisation rates demonstrated in their study. They suggest this may be due to poor reporting of episodes - unlikely in the case of polio, diphtheria and tetanus - or to the relative isolation of Travellers from settled communities.

A study in Scotland suggests an alternative reason for this phenomenon: despite 56% of their sample having no recollection of immunisation, 83.5% had anti-bodies to polio, 81% to diphtheria and 50.5% to tetanus (Riding, 1985).

Frequent visits to sites of all kinds during the project led the SHV to observe the high incidence of accidents to children in the home, especially of burns and scalds, both of which were much more prevalent than in the settled population. Interview evidence suggests that Traveller parents are reactive to accidents, rather than proactive or aware of preventive measures. Lack of access to even simple awareness and preventive literature, for the reasons suggested above, mean an inappropriate use of the acute services and accident and emergency departments.

Crout (1988), who undertook similar studies in Walsall, points out that to counter-balance the increased risks of environmental physical risk factors among Travellers, there was a lower incidence of non-accidental injury to Traveller children. The Avon project demonstrated that of all the families coming within the SHV purview between May 1990 and November 1992, one had a child on the 'at risk' register, and two were known to be 'cause for concern'. Considerable time and involvement by the SHV was devoted to escorting Gypsy children to clinics and out-patient appointments, a function which expanded as the confidence of families to 'try' these services built up, following preliminary project work with them.

Male and adult health issues

Whilst the emphasis of the project was on maternal and child care activities, there was an inevitable involvement by the SHV in the health problems of other members of travelling families.

The Walsall study (Crout, 1988) had produced evidence of a high rate of cardiovascular disease among males in Gypsy and Traveller groups compared with the indigenous population. Pahl and Vaile (1988) report that life expectancy for a Traveller is 48 years, which has led the SHV to recommend that in future stages of the Avon project, attention should be given to nutritional advice, smoking, alcohol abuse and the management of stress.

Health promotion work during the project period was planned jointly with other health workers and the Travellers themselves. Utilising existing women's groups and informal networks among Traveller families, information and advice was offered on safety equipment in the home, on drug abuse and, in addition, a keep fit class was introduced.

Avon Traveller Women's Group provided funding for a trained physiotherapist to lead these sessions. Such meetings enabled informal discussion to develop around health issues, although the SHV reported some reluctance to engage with these topics. The physical and social activities were, however, much appreciated.

Some further health education of an informal kind was developed within the activities of the Bristol Playbus, a pre-school scheme which visits sites on a regular basis. At these sessions, issues of dental health, road safety and accidents in the home were introduced, and were well received. This suggests that the level of receptivity of health topics is related to the possibility of their taking place on 'home ground'. As a result, the SHV was led to recommend a mobile health education facility for site visits in the future development of the scheme.

Summary

As a result of the SHV activities during the project period, a number of key issues for developing better delivery of health care services to Traveller groups can be identified. It is evident that the most pressing need is for safe, legal sites with water, sanitation and electricity. This should allow a greater possibility of success in developing access to primary preventive services, screening and targeted campaigns dealing with specific issues such as drug abuse, diet and safety. The availability of hand-held records will be an important aid to continuity of health care, allied to improved access to secondary care services. The availability of social benefits and the development of out-reach services for welfare rights, social work and family support is important.

Key tasks for the SHV in future phases of the project will need to be in facilitating the use of services, operating a domiciliary immunisation service and the promotion of networking among other agencies. The growth of coordinated approaches to travelling families, with the involvement of education, site management and health workers is an important priority for progress in this field. The raising of awareness of staff in these agencies and in health centres, especially those such as receptionists who are 'gate-keepers', is crucial to greater understanding of the problems faced by mobile families.

At the end of the initial phase of the Avon project, the SHV made a number of recommendations for the future, and these included better administrative support, a mobile clinic which could go onto unauthorised sites as well as official ones, and a nominated physician in public health to have special responsibility for liaison with other services.

Other recommendations include more sites, better services to unofficial sites and the need to consult with health workers before evictions take place. The SHV urged, for example, that no eviction should take place in which a pregnant woman or new-born baby was involved.

Discussion

This glimpse of the current state of health care services as received by a range of travelling families is, in a sense, one more piece of the jigsaw provided by various studies of a similar kind.

As Pahl and Vaile (1988) point out, there has been a growing recognition over a number of years that members of most ethnic and cultural minorities can face particular difficulties in getting access to health and welfare services. Whilst many local initiatives have aimed at closing this gap for black and Asian people, little attention has been paid to the peculiar problems of groups who, by their very lifestyle, choose not to stay in one place.

But in fact there have been a number of studies, dating back to the early 1980s, which have argued that the provision of legal and properly serviced stopping places are the first and most basic requirement for delivering good health care.

This is not to argue that Travellers should stop travelling if they want full integration and participation in the welfare state apparatus; but rather to accept that as British society becomes more heterogeneous and culturally diverse, it may be necessary to adapt the services on offer and the method of delivery to meet the needs of differing cultural groups.

In other words the National Health Service needs to recognise what Boushel (1994) terms the "cultural inappropriateness" of many of the resources available, and widen the options, especially to the women and children of nomadic families.

This may require that the staff and managers in education, health and social service agencies have to do more jointly, to create a partnership between service users and front-line workers; to build, in Boushel's formulation, an "anti-oppressive and culturally sensitive" value base for their work.

Nowhere is this more important than in the field of maternal health services and child care, especially in the context of the Children Act 1989. Despite recent theoretical developments in anti-discrimination and user empowerment, the Avon project makes it clear that much needs to be done practically in developing skills for working with groups and communities.

Contradictions abound. A study of Irish Travellers has shown that infant mortality and still-births are twice as high as in the settled population, whilst 'un-housed' Travellers of all ages are seven times more prone to fatal accident (O'Higgins, 1992). This study also looked at child care and found that the children of Irish Travellers living on unofficial sites are more likely to be received into care than settled children, and face much more difficulty in keeping contact with their families once received into care. This suggests that children of Travellers are less valued by both state and community than other children.

On the other hand it can be argued, as Boushel (1994) suggests, that Traveller children are in some ways better protected by their communities' shared values of family life and close kinship links. Certainly observation suggests that most nomadic groups will go to considerable lengths to tolerate socially unacceptable behaviour by young members of the group.

In most of the earlier studies, as in the Avon case study, those with direct involvement in the delivery of basic health care have argued that safe, well-serviced sites are the essential pre-requisite to improving the access.

In Walsall (Crout, 1987), in East Anglia, Sheffield and East London (Cornwell, 1984), and in Tunbridge Wells and Birmingham (Bell and Malia, 1992), the researchers have argued that in the absence of adequate numbers of sites, the emphasis must be on organisational responses, such as out-reach work, mobile clinics and a continuity of service. Most of the authors have emphasised the importance of building confidence among Travellers that they will be treated on their own terms, and assurance that because they do not conform to middle-class professional values, they will not be rejected or humiliated.

Continuity of care in a mobile population leads to arguments for hand-held records and the possibility that travelling families should be given their own health records to be taken with them wherever they go.

Most studies also argue for a nominated 'Gypsy specialist', usually a health visitor, who can coordinate all the other services in that area and work alongside GPs, education and social work staff. Not the least of the tasks, as Cornwell (1984) argues, is to combat prejudice and discriminatory reactions among staff who deal with Travellers.

There is, however, a danger in this strategy and especially in placing the emphasis on providing specialist workers and special services. It could be argued that this approach singles out travelling groups as 'a problem', and by implication sees their lifestyle as somehow to blame for poor service delivery.

Durward (1990), whose study of Traveller mothers and babies was sponsored by the Maternity Alliance, suggests that before embarking on any initiatives, there should be careful consultation and collaboration with representatives of Traveller organisations. She suggests there is no need to demonstrate that nomadic groups are unhealthier or more at risk than settled people in order to justify essential services which are their right.

In this view, simply living in a hostile society which manifests its rejection on a daily basis creates additional stresses on mothers and children, so that specially designed responses end up addressing the effects rather than the causes.

The problem with this approach is that, as the Avon case study shows, there are vast differences of culture, history and lifestyle between Gypsies, Irish Travellers and New Age Travellers, which make attempts at collaboration and the establishment of a common view about health or sites or anything else a somewhat daunting proposition. And whilst legal sites are so scarce, the very precariousness of the nomadic lifestyle is a practical hurdle of some magnitude.

In the face of the diversity of these groups, it is perhaps sensible to view the provision of specialist approaches to Traveller health care as some kind of 'bridge' aimed at building trust and increasing knowledge (Pahl and Vaile, 1988). In this way, and over time, the beneficial effects of primary care, immunisation and antenatal services, introduced alongside better education services and more sites, may allow Travellers to receive a comprehensive health care service.

The fact that Pahl and Vaile were able to demonstrate so clearly that those who exist on illegal sites with no basic facilities were significantly less well served, is a powerful argument for re-thinking the approach to site provision embodied in the 1994 Criminal Justice Act, about which this book is mainly concerned.

The Avon case studies in Chapters 4 and 5 give real-life evidence of the way in which the British welfare state and its services impact on the encampments and roadsides of Avon. They reinforce the view that the experience is much the same for travelling groups wherever they happen to stop.

But they also illustrate vividly the contradictions and confusions which exist both in the bureaucracies and in the daily lives of those who work with Travellers. The hard facts are never quite the same between one agency and another; the figures are riddled with uncertainty and - as one might expect with Gypsies - tackling the problems is so often about dealing with a moving target. Just as you think you have the measure of a problem, it subtly changes.

Thus, the scale and type of problem which Avon Education Department thought it had identified is different in a number of ways from that which the health authority perceived. Only at the fringes were the two agencies able to collaborate, and that was much more to do with aware professionals than it was with policy coherence or collaboration at agency level.

The Avon studies illustrate, too, the limits to progress when there is no overall strategy or corporate plan to provide services. The lack of political will which prevented the construction of legal sites for Travellers until 1994 was ultimately the reason why both health and education services, fuelled by a very positive professional will, had a limited effect. There is another kind of ambivalence which peeps tantalisingly from the pages of these studies: that of the travelling families themselves towards the various agents of the state who turn up on their makeshift sites. Yes, they want their children to learn to read, but no, they do not necessarily want them registered, listed and irrevocably tied into the bureaucratic machinery of formal education. Yes, they want some kinds of preventive health care, but not others. Yes, they want to be able to go to a regular local doctor, but they are much happier turning up at the accident and emergency department of the local hospital when treatment is needed. A women's group ostensibly formed to promote health education and to offer birth control advice, actually became a keep fit and social gathering.

All those who work with Gypsies need to understand the nature of this enigmatic stance, which they are liable to meet in attempting to deliver services or to befriend the Gypsy. It stems from a number of sources, both social and cultural. On the one hand, Gypsies have a genuine desire to preserve a distinct and separate existence without having to be excluded from the facilities and resources to which they have a right. On the other hand, there is a well-founded wariness of officialdom of all kinds, which has usually been the bearer of bad news or has made unpalatable demands.

At its most sublime, this phenomenon is the expression of an incompatibility between the Gypsy and the state which originates in ageless cultural experience and from a strain of anarchic non-conformity which is inimical to order and control. In practice it is much more mundane, crude and antagonistic; but it is the basis on which Travellers are willing to treat.

The lesson of the case studies is that we must accept the terms of the treaty and learn to ground our relationships in an understanding of that fundamental proposition: 'we are who we are'.

six

THE RADICAL DEPARTURE: THE CRIMINAL JUSTICE AND PUBLIC ORDER BILL

Earlier chapters have traced the life-cycle of the government's policy for Gypsy site provision over 25 years of its history, and by means of case studies we have seen how the 1968 Act and allied attempts to provide social services have impacted at local level, and on Gypsies and Travellers.

It is now necessary to examine in detail the events which followed the startling announcement, through a Conservative central office election press release, that the policy enshrined in the Act was to be terminated.

Whilst it is not clear what prompted the decision or what factors emerged following the 1991 House of Commons debate, in which support for the continuation of the policy was unanimous, it is evident that the change of direction was essentially ideological.

A new junior minister, Tony Baldry, had been appointed and the fact of a general election had no doubt prompted a review of those issues which would carry electoral popularity.   Since public expenditure control was at the heart of the 1992 election debate, and every budget came under Treasury scrutiny immediately following the re-election of the Major government, it is also evident that the main elements of the proposals for a new approach to Gypsy problems included a shift of financial emphasis from public provision to private self-help.

The election press release had suggested that the number of Gypsy caravans had grown by 30% since 1981 and that despite a 67% increase in official pitches there were between 2,000 and 5,000 New Age Travellers camping illegally in England and Wales, in addition to the 4,000 Gypsies not yet provided with official stopping places.

It went on to blame the 1968 Act for not only failing to solve the problems, but exacerbating them and placing an 'open-ended' commitment on local authorities. Relying more on election debating points than policy analysis, it condemned the disruptive effects of large-scale illegal camping and promised swifter and tougher action to remove those stopping illegally.

Consultation

Within two months of the new government being returned, these proposals had hardened into a more coherent set of proposals which were contained in a consultation paper to local authorities and others on the reform of the 1968 Act (DoE, 1992). The paper argued that both demographic and economic circumstances had changed since the inception of the Act. Numbers had grown from an estimated 3,400 families mentioned in the 1965 research to nearer 10,000; other kinds of itinerant had become prominent, complicating the issues and raising questions of who came within the definition of 'Gypsies and other Travellers'. It argued that traditional patterns of travel and employment had given way to new.

The link between unofficial camping and petty crime and the ineffectiveness of the eviction processes were stressed. The paper proposed:

- repealing the 1968 Act provisions placing a duty on authorities to provide sufficient sites, and substituting a discretionary power so to do;

- repealing the secretary of state's powers to designate areas and to direct authorities;

- encouraging Gypsies to move into private and public sector housing;

- withdrawal of the 100% capital grant from general availability, targeting it instead at the minister's discretion, to stress areas or those authorities already under direction to make new sites.

Proposals for considerably tougher measures to remove illegal parkers were outlined and the consultation paper also sought views on the suggestion that seizure of caravans was likely to be more effective than monetary fines, but only as a last resort. It was further suggested that the vehicle would be returned once the owner had satisfied the court that a legal place had been found to put it.

The consultation paper argued that earlier relaxations of green belt planning policies which allowed sites to be placed in rural areas were a "privilege" which should be withdrawn; in future Gypsies would be encouraged to provide funding for their own sites "on the same terms as anyone else", seeking planning consent in the normal way.

The paper suggested again that the 1968 Act was an open-ended commitment which undermined Gypsies' responsibility to provide for themselves and there was an underlying assumption that, in due course, Gypsies would become home owners and relinquish the itinerant way of life.

But, even at this early stage of policy reformation, and as we have noted in earlier legislation, it is again evident that there are uniquely threatening elements directed at the Gypsy and Traveller which have no parallel in other kinds of cultural context. For example, the suggestion that someone's home might be 'confiscated' for what is, in effect, a parking offence, might be considered draconian in the extreme, and would affect only the itinerant. To think of the consequences of a similar sanction against someone in the settled population, perhaps puts the suggestion into perspective.

The whole tone of the paper, with its emphasis on private solutions is, in a sense, proposing the *embourgeoisement* of a population for whom that term could be considered somewhat inappropriate.

In seeking clues to the origins of what the consultation paper itself called a "significant shift of policy", we are assisted by two short parliamentary debates which occurred whilst the consultation was underway.

In a debate on a private member's Bill in February 1993, and again during an adjournment debate in July, opportunities arose to judge both the government's intentions and the mood of members, to the issues raised in the new approach. These debates also allowed some of the darker prejudices against itinerant minorities to surface. Thus, Mr Sykes, the member for Scarborough:

> The plain, unvarnished truth about New Age Travellers and people like them is that, in many cases, they are dirty, lazy drop-outs, whose dedication to their way of life extends no

further than the nearest benefit office, followed closely by the nearest pub. (Hansard, 1993a and 1993b)

For Mr Sykes, those who stand up for the rights of Travellers are standing up for loafers and spongers, hiding their position behind a veil of wishing to preserve Gypsies' way of life at all costs.

But powerful criticism of the minister's new approach came from fellow Conservatives. The member for Hampshire south-west, Sir David Mitchell, questioned the logic of withdrawing the duty to provide sites, when it was acknowledged that more sites were needed; he wondered how, when local authorities had been unable to get possible sites through the planning system, Gypsies themselves would succeed.

It emerged in this debate that virtually all the responses to the consultation paper had been negative or had rejected the proposals for change. The minister had declined to make responses publicly available, but had simply published a list of those who had responded. It was suggested that bodies such as the Country Landowners Association, the Council for the Preservation of Rural England and the National Farmers Union had all questioned the wisdom of repealing the 1968 Act duty. Such bodies, who might have been expected to take a supportive view, saw no benefit in stopping the impetus to new official sites.

Local authorities throughout Britain, together with all the Gypsy support organisations, had, it was alleged, taken the view expressed by Hampshire County Council, that the government's proposals would ensure that prospects for resolution of the problems were likely to worsen.

The junior minister, Mr Baldry, however, thought that to publish the responses would be unhelpful because so many of them had misunderstood the government intention. He stressed that, with new planning guidance to local authorities, and a requirement to make provision in local plans for sites, the planning system is "perfectly capable" of making the necessary provision. If an authority unreasonably refused consent to a private site application, "an appeal is possible".

The public response to the consultation paper gave every indication that most of those with an interest in the issue wished to see the existing system strengthened rather than abolished.

The Criminal Justice Bill

The legislative opportunity to introduce the government's ideas came with the introduction of the Criminal Justice and Public Order Bill, which, according to the Queen's speech at the beginning of the new parliament, was intended to give priority to law and order and to allow the courts to deal more effectively with offenders by improving the criminal law.

Part V of the new Bill encompassed strong new enforcement powers directed mainly against the New Age Travellers and the open air music festivals or 'raves', and the illegal occupation of fields for such events, but with equally direct effects on traditional travelling families. There were four main proposals which had the effect of bringing to an end the 25 years of consensual policy in regard to provision for Gypsies and Travellers:

- The repeal of part II of the 1968 Act, removing the duty on local authorities to provide sites, and abolishing the government grant for constructing Gypsy caravan sites.

- An extended power for local authorities to direct unauthorised campers to leave land, including any land forming part of a highway, any other unoccupied land, or any land occupied without the owner's consent. It would become a criminal offence for anyone so directed to refuse to leave, or to return to it within three months.

- An extended power to magistrate's courts to make orders authorising local authorities to enter land and remove vehicles and property, if persons are present in contravention of a direction to leave. *not yet in force* .

- A strengthening of the powers contained in the Public Order Act 1986 (section 39), giving the police power to direct trespassers to leave if they have damaged the land itself (as distinct from property on it), or if they have six vehicles. It also extends the application of this section to common land, highway verges, byways, green lanes and other minor highways, and includes new police powers to remove vehicles.

Although a full analysis of the responses to the consultation paper has never been published by the DoE, and the 'digest' which ministers said was to be published has not appeared, it is nevertheless possible to ascertain the views which local authorities expressed. Research was undertaken by ACERT and is set out in Table 12, which clearly indicates that the vast majority did not feel that the new proposals were workable, or that withdrawal of funding would be practicable. It is also clear that over half of authorities wished to see a statutory duty to provide sites retained, and a distinction to be made between New Age Travellers and traditional Travellers and Gypsies.

Table 12: The responses of local authorities involved with setting up and running sites to the August 1992 consultation document

	County councils (46 responses)	London boroughs/ metropolitan authorities (39 responses)	Districts (239 responses)
Government proposals do not provide workable solutions	93%	92%	71%
Distinguish between Gypsies and New Age Travellers	67%	20%	38%
Retain statutory duty	56%	56%	48% [51%]
Retain 100% funding	73% [78%]	61% [66%]	53% [55%]

Note: Percentages in square brackets include those by implication

Source: Derived from ACERT, briefing note, April 1994

The considerable unease and widespread rejection of these proposals which had been expressed during the consultation period were now translated to an extensive lobbying during the passage of the measure. It appeared that, apart from a withdrawal by the government of the suggestion of 'confiscating' caravans and the removal of a suggestion that Travellers might be assisted financially to move into housing, virtually no modifications had been made to the proposals set out in consultation documents.

It could be argued that to bring forward modifications to Gypsy policy in a Bill dealing with criminal justice is itself to exacerbate existing prejudice against the whole travelling population. However, more specific criticisms came from such bodies as Save the Children Fund, the National Housing and Town Planning Council, civil liberties groups, the police and private law firms.

Scotland's chief constables raised the practical problems of introducing a concept of 'aggravated trespass' as a criminal offence and suggested that it was both unnecessary and would be difficult to implement.

The National Housing and Town Planning Council expressed serious misgivings about both the motives and measures in the Bill, and the apparent conflation of two distinct issues: the unlawful occupation of land on the one hand, and the site provision policies for Gypsy families on the other.

In many other careful contributions to the debate, the key issue highlighted was the questionable tactic of harnessing public outrage at the illegal and disruptive activities of those who attended unlicenced 'rave' parties, some of whom were New Age Travellers but most of whom were not, to limit public sympathy for the provision of sites for traditional travelling families. The National Housing and Town Planning Council was also among a number of commentators which questioned the wisdom of repealing the key provisions of the 1968 Act before a full programme of sites had been completed.

Even *The Spectator* characterised the Bill as repressive and unacceptable: "Any Bill which makes Gypsies into criminals and threatens nomadic tradition, is oppressive" (Courtauld, 1994).

There was little opposition to the suggestion that more sites should be encouraged by the voluntary action of Travellers themselves, and indeed the National Gypsy Council is itself actively pursuing that policy. However, most expressed considerable scepticism about the ability of the new planning guidance to facilitate this end.

The Save the Children Fund stressed the impact on the health and welfare of children which would be caused by mass disruption, eviction and an increase in powers to move caravans on. Liberty, the civil rights campaign, announced a plan to test the legality of the Bill's provisions in the European Court of Human Rights, with particular reference to the perceived surveillance by police of New Age Traveller groups and the introduction in the Bill of a new power for police to apprehend Travellers on the basis of a reasonable suspicion that they were travelling to an unlicensed 'rave' or music festival.

The Bill's passage through both Commons and Lords was both controversial and passionately argued, throughout the spring and summer of 1994 although, as a minor part of a much wider set of measures, part V received limited attention and only sporadic coverage in the press.

An alliance of bodies, including ACERT, Save the Children Fund and Liberty lobbied on specific and detailed clauses, a campaign which was instrumental in the defeat, in the House of Lords, of the Bill's intention to abolish the duties of local authorities to go on providing sites.

At the eleventh hour, with the Bill at report stage in the House of Lords, a significant amendment was agreed to postpone for five years the repeal of the 1968 Act. If agreed, the duty on local authorities to provide sites and the 100% government grant to the capital costs of new sites would go on until 1999. Designation would continue as would the ministerial duty to direct recalcitrant authorities. Ominously for the government, most of those speakers in favour were government supporters.

Lord Stanley of Alderly argued that this would give more time to complete the sites programme and to judge whether the new 'private sector option' was going to work. Another government supporter, Baroness Faithfull, fearing a similar social catastrophe as that in the 18th century highland clearances, said it would allow time for careful thought and planning of the new regime. Lord Tenby said: "If the existing provisions are passed there will be a duty on authorities to enforce them with all the attendant stresses and miseries which they will bring to the Gypsies, with regard to education, health and peace of mind. How can it do otherwise than to lead to more illegal camping and greater friction within countryside communities?" (Hansard, 1994).

In this debate, there was not only a quiet anger, but a sense of the iniquity of the government's proposals, summed up perhaps most trenchantly in the words of Lord Irvine:

> There is humbug at the heart of the government's policy. This humbug is not simply that they must know that what they are suggesting is unrealistic as a solution to the problem of unauthorised sites; it is also that at the same time as they suggest that private site provision is the solution on which we should reply, they are making such provision more difficult

by altering national planning policies. The real effect of the legislation, which they dare not openly avow, is to make those who have no lawful place to reside in their vehicles disappear through the imposition of criminal sanctions. (Hansard, 1994)

With a significant number of Conservative peers voting against the government, the amendment was agreed by 133 votes to 104. For connoisseurs, the Lords debate of 11 July is a classic example of the demolition, piece by piece, of the government's case, grounded as it is in ideological rather than rational or practical premises; quietly, without drama or great oratory, accumulating over 45 minutes of polite debate, a devastating critique emerges of the illogic, the impracticability and simply the ill-thought-out consequences of part V of the Bill (Hansard, 1994).

But the underlying opposition to the Criminal Justice and Public Order Bill lay in much deeper philosophical/legal objections to its intentions. It was argued that it contravened the European Convention on Human Rights, to which the UK government is a signatory. Specifically, article 8 of the Convention which protects the right to respect for private and family life, and article 14 which protects against discrimination in the enjoyment of rights under the Convention, would, it was said, be breached. The Commission, in 1981 (9278/81 and 9415/81: G&E v Norway 35 D&R 30), had stated that: "under Article 8 a minority group is, in principle, entitled to claim the right to respect for the particular lifestyle it may lead, as being 'private life', 'family life' or 'home'".

In the opinion of one learned counsel, the Bill as enacted (or even if there had been a delay of five years in the abolition of the duty to provide sites) will mean that Gypsies will be forced to abandon their culture and caravan living and assimilate, or face a battery of laws which will make it virtually impossible to continue lawful caravan living and expose them to criminal penalties if they cannot stop on a plot with planning permission (Save the Children, 1994). Lobbyists argued that the inherent improbability of sufficient provision being made through private initiative and the planning system was a major motivation more than 25 years ago for the enactment of the 1968 Act.

Professionals and lobbyists agreed that leaving all to the planning system will fail to provide anything like sufficient sites to enable Gypsies to continue lawfully to reside in caravans, giving rise to potential breaches of the Convention on Human Rights.

Whilst earlier attempts by some Gypsies to seek protection under articles 8 and 14 had been held inadmissible by the European Court, because the 1968 Act established a duty to provide sites, it was argued in the Lords debate that, under the regime of the new Criminal Justice and Public Order Bill as originally drafted, the duty would no longer exist.   It would, though, still mean that challenges against the new measure would have to be fought on a case by case basis - a long-term war of attrition which Gypsies and Travellers are signally ill-equipped to pursue.

The Committee of Ministers of the EU has adopted recommendations opposing discrimination against Gypsies.   For example, Rec R(81)1 states: "In their law and practice regarding the movement and residence of persons, states should refrain from any measure which would lead to discrimination against nomads for reasons of their nomadic lifestyle".

Despite all this, in November 1994 the Criminal Justice Act received the Royal Assent, with the provisions of part V untouched. The Lords amendments were rejected by the Commons and the original clauses re-inserted.   The end of a 25 year period of policy consensus for the public support of residential sites for travelling people had come, in a way that few had expected and most would have thought impossible.

In summary then, the argument is that a wholly inadequate provision of sites will result under the Act.   If this proves correct, Gypsy families and those others who choose to follow a similar mode of living will be forced to choose between assimilation by living in houses, and illegality and criminalisation if they attempt to continue caravan living.   Such a choice hits at the heart of traditional Gypsy culture and justifies the concerns discussed above about respect for minority rights.   It should be said, however, by way of putting the argument in perspective, that such a dilemma is not different from that which has faced generations of Gypsies in the United Kingdom, from the time when they faced a choice between emigration and beheading.   Somehow or other, they accommodate each new threat, be it extermination or assimilation, with a degree of equanimity to be envied.   Is it because they understand, better than others, that draconian measures are more for the consumption of the established majority, than for execution against themselves?

It has been argued, indeed demonstrated, in the above pages that the impetus for change, based upon no logical or researched case that can be discerned, has been posited upon an ideological view of personal responsibility and perceived 'privilege' for previous Gypsy policy. But it has been driven through by the harnessing of a justified public anger at one phenomenon (the actions of some participants in large-scale, open air music festivals and the disruptive consequences which can result) to the latent prejudice and discrimination which has, through the ages, been aimed at traditional Gypsies and Travellers. These events, characterised as 'raves', are defined for the first time in legislation as "a gathering in the open air of 100 or more people at which amplified music is played in the night and which by reason of its loudness and duration is likely to cause serious distress to local inhabitants". The evidence to date is that many people who travel to such events do so in caravans, but that virtually none are traditional Gypsies or Travellers.

seven

THE POLITICS OF PREJUDICE

So far, in the earlier part of this volume, we have followed the sempiternal Gypsy journey, tracing both the historical and the modern relationship of Gypsies and other Travellers to the British state. It is a journey which has provoked response after antagonistic response, each, despite apparently being of its time, remaining curiously consistent down the ages. Similar themes occur and re-occur: threat and sanction, attempts at assimilation, attempts to identify 'genuine' Gypsies whilst condemning 'pretended egyptians' which is what Henry VIII would have called New Age Travellers.

Even when, in 1968, the state acknowledged the legitimacy of a way of life quite alien to the notions of the house-dwelling majority and began to provide sites, still the law included unique prejudicial sanctions which were aimed at those very elements of travelling life which make it different from any other.

In the words of one Traveller, it is as if the Gorgio is saying: "Of course we must cater for your interesting differences, but we must encourage you, to the point of coercion, to stop being different - or at least make it as difficult as possible" (Hawes, 1994).

In this chapter the aim is to isolate and examine the engines of prejudice, the mechanisms of discrimination; in a sense, to hold them up to the light, look at the subtle changes they undergo with each airing. If, between 1968 and 1994, these contradictions were surrounded in ambiguity, in the Criminal Justice and Public Order Act 1994 they are crystal clear and sharply articulated.

The specific manifestations of such prejudice, as it is expressed in legislation, centre on the concept of 'designation' and in the attempts to define who is a Gypsy, and in other, less specific aspects of the web of legislation. But before examining these in detail, and in order to facilitate understanding, it is as well to consider first some theoretical concepts of the nature of prejudice.

The nature of prejudice

There are a number of theoretical constructs which might illuminate the process by which social stigmatisation becomes formally recognised, structurally supported oppression. However, not all of them seem easily to explain the particular issues we are attempting to illuminate.

Exploitation theory, for example, as expounded by Marx, suggests that race prejudice is a social attitude propagated by an exploiting class for the purpose of stigmatising a minority group as inferior, so that exploitation of the group or its resources can be justified (Cox, 1948).

From an historical perspective race prejudice has grown from the colonial movements, rationalising 'inferiority' as a mask for slavery, oppression and exploitation. Cox argues that class difference (ie the exploiter/exploited relationship) is the foundation of all prejudice, and that all talk about racial, ethnic or cultural factors is a verbal mask.

This emphasis, however, ignores the psychological factors, and also that Gypsies and Travellers have never presented an economic challenge to society, nor have they any resources which could be exploited.

More relevantly, for our purposes, the socio-cultural emphasis places importance upon the total social context in which prejudicial attitudes develop, examining the traditions that lead to conflict, the relative upward mobility of 'in-groups' and 'out-groups', and the phenomenon of urbanisation as a cause of ethnic prejudice - the loss of community and personal relationships. This argument suggests that the insecurity and impersonal nature of city life places stress upon the basic ethno-centrism of every group.

Thus every cultural problem reaches the individual only through the mediation of his or her group so that social education allows each of us to appreciate every object from the standpoint of the group view of it. This view tells us that we cannot help but adopt the judgements of our ancestors, through what Allport calls a "screen of tradition" (Allport, 1982).

Even more pertinent to the issue of Gypsies is the scapegoat theory, which assumes that anger, once engendered, is displaced upon some relevant victim. It suggests that the instinctive human response to frustration is aggressive assertiveness and anger which is directed to available objects rather than logical ones. Gypsies are often 'available'.

Writers who approach the study of prejudice from a phenomenological point of view argue that a person's conduct proceeds immediately from his or her view of the situation confronting them. In other words, one's response to the world conforms to one's definitions of the world. One attacks the members of another group because one perceives them as repulsive, annoying or threatening. In this formulation, what one perceives or believes, however crudely stereotypical, is the spring of reaction.

Of course, we must acknowledge that there are genuine differences between groups that provoke hostility; in most cases, however, differences are less than they are imagined to be. Reputations are not so much earned as gratuitously thrust upon a group.

There are ethnic or national traits which are perceived by others as actually menacing, provoking reasonable hostility. This has led some writers to emphasise an interaction theory, in which some hostility is provoked by the object, and some by essentially irrational stimuli such as scapegoating, guilt displacement, and culturally-based prejudice.

A new generation of academic writers, perhaps responding to the developing multi-culturalism of British society, has taken these issues forward, grounding its analysis in concepts of the politics of difference. Ethnicity, gender and disability are all at the heart of this debate, as is the difference represented by nomadism, whether manifested in the Gypsies and Travellers or the more recent New Age groups.

In all of these kinds of difference, the importance for public policy and for those who administer it, is the way in which the state and its services interact with the groups said to be 'different' and provide the services they need.

In the struggle to remove elements of discrimination and to neuter overt prejudice from these interactions, writers such as Solomos (1989), Gordon (1992) and Husband (1982) have stressed the ways in which difficulties are given cultural meaning so that, for example, Gypsies and Travellers, who would argue that their social identity is recognisably different, are therefore disadvantaged in terms of wider perception of social structure. As Gordon (1992) puts it, they experience a "different reality".

What the case studies undertaken for this volume confirm is the tentative suggestion by Husband (1982) that there is a link between the analysis of deprivation on the one hand and its policy implications on the other. But they also show that the gap between sociological analysis and political action is vast.

At one level, at least, the aims of social policy are concerned with issues such as the securing of rights, justice and meeting needs; but as Husband (1982) argues, these objectives do not co-exist comfortably alongside notions of freedom. Indeed, the account of the experience of Gypsies and Travellers related in these pages, placed in an historical context, would seem to confirm what Solomos (1989) calls racialisation as a political process.

In examining these issues as they emerge in public policy responses to Gypsies, other travelling groups and the more recent New Age nomads, it is possible to see a number of theoretical elements of prejudice made manifest.

But it is not the purpose of this work to develop these arguments except to register the central importance of the debate in analysing the real life relationships between the Gypsy and the state, and in attempting to understand the mechanisms which allow cultural prejudice and legalised discrimination to become enshrined in legal instruments such as the Criminal Justice Act 1994.

In British policy it is of course true that there is a formal recognition of cultural rights and anti-racist values, which are acknowledged for example in the Swann Report on education services. These approaches have resulted in important growth in literacy, specialist teaching and social advances. Race relations law provides some protection and the 1968 Act has been the basis for a vast legalisation of Gypsy and Traveller life (Acton, 1991).

On the other hand, as Acton argues, respect for Gypsy culture is still fundamentally conceived within a racist ideology, defining 'true' Gypsy (or traditional Traveller): "These are guidelines for building better ghettos, not for implementing human rights" (Acton, 1991).

Designation

Similarly, the designation provision in the 1968 Act confers discriminatory powers of summary eviction against 'surplus' Gypsy caravans. Gypsies have argued endlessly that this makes them the only ethnic group subject to official and legal quotas as to where and how many may live in particular locations. Designated districts and counties are, in effect, subject to ethnic cleansing. Throughout its existence, the 1968 Act was, in Acton's view, fatally undermined by this device, bringing extra harassment powers to the authority in the area designated (Acton, 1991).

It has not been disputed that this device was created as a 'reward' for authorities who were willing to provide official sites, and in most cases it was achieved for making a level of provision which bore no relation, necessarily, to the actual level of need, as related to the number of Gypsies known to use an area. Nevertheless, faced with a distinct lack of enthusiasm to respond to the policy, designation must have seemed a reasonable device *pour encourager les autres.*

London boroughs and former county boroughs were required to find only 15 pitches in order to be designated. For others, it was a matter of constructing a site or two and then making a case to the DoE, in most cases without too much difficulty. By 1993 62% of authorities had achieved designation (DoE, 1991c).

The DoE itself recognised the extreme discriminatory effect of this device; in circular 57/78 it advised authorities: "Powers that flow from designation are severely discriminatory against one group of people and their use is justifiable only on the basis that the duty of the responsible local authority with regard to that group has been fully implemented" (DoE, 1978).

But with the advent of the Criminal Justice and Public Order Act 1994, the overt discrimination has become wider and more forcefully expressed. Lloyd (1993) has suggested that not only are the new measures likely to be counter-productive, even on the government's own terms, but they represent a blatantly discriminatory and oppressive attitude: "a scapegoating of Travellers and a denial of civil and human rights".

Lloyd argues that taking into account the relaxation of border controls in Europe, the government's aim is to pre-empt any possibility of movement of European Travellers to Britain. "These proposals demonstrate how a perceived threat to law and order can be managed by using the victimised as scapegoats" (Lloyd, 1993, p 84).

If this assessment seems somewhat over-dramatic, it is not difficult to find, in the pages of Hansard, expressions of attitudes among politicians which support its judgement. Thus, the home secretary, referring to the 'peace convoy' of 1986: "It resembles nothing so much as a band of medieval brigands who have no respect for the law or the rights of others" (Hansard, 1986). John Carlisle, MP, in the same debate said: "The time has come for Gypsies to be banished to the wilderness they deserve".

Comments of this kind from members of the government and their supporters underpin the view that since the hardening of policy appears not to be based on any known research or evidence, it is important to look for the ideological sources from which it springs. Okely (1983) perhaps comes closest: "Those who confront the prevailing order, those who demonstrate alternative possibilities in economic spheres, in ways of being and thinking, those who appear as powerful symbols, must, it seems, be contained and controlled". This is a notion almost identical to that quoted in Chapter 2, by which the Elizabethan authorities sought to penalise the 'Egyptians'. It is perhaps the powerful symbol of unfettered, anarchic freedom, which Gypsies represent in a world regulated, bureaucratised and urban, that so unsettles our state lawmakers and local officers.

Gypsies and the planning system

The network of legal structures and regulations which constitute the British planning system are another example, in the view of some commentators, of the law placing uniquely prejudicial constraints on the Gypsy and Traveller lifestyle, bedevilling attempts by authorities and Gypsies to make new sites. To complement the new Criminal Justice and Public Order Act, new planning guidelines were issued to authorities in DoE circular 1/94. They highlight the Kafka-like web through which anyone now wishing to provide their own site will have to weave.

In 1977 planning authorities were advised that green belt restraint policies could be relaxed to allow Gypsy sites in rural locations close to urban fringes; the grounds on which this move was posited were that since so much opposition was engendered against applicants for sites in more residential areas, it could be difficult to prevent unauthorised camping in less suitable locations. DoE circular 57/78 said "sites suitable in other respects may conflict with green belt or other planning policies". But the special need to accommodate Gypsies - and the consequences of not accommodating them - should be taken into account as a material consideration in reading planning decisions. However, in the debate on the new Bill this was seen as a 'privileged position' for Gypsies, which could no longer be defended. The planning guidance reinforces this stance and means a doubly prejudicial landscape for the aspiring Gypsy applicant for a planning consent.

First, the unrestrained prejudice which Gypsies experience at the hands of the settled majority inevitably manifests itself as unreasoned and extreme objection to any proposal to establish a site, the vehemence of the opposition generally being out of all proportion to objections on any logical planning grounds that may exist. This is a fundamental impediment which will damn any application at the outset, and may prevent the possibility of meeting the government's wish that these applications should be treated "on the same grounds as other development".

The second relates to the actual provisions of the legislation, embedded in guidance notes and development plans. The absence of detailed requirements in structure, unitary development and local plans, ie to state specifically where the development of Gypsy sites will be permitted, makes any application a lottery. It is important that specific criteria and locations are set down.

Writing in 1982 Home pointed out that criteria then existing, which state that sites should have reasonable access to shops, schools and essential services, but should not be too close to substantial residential development, posed a 'Catch 22' situation, justifying the refusal of any application. If sites are near shops and services then they are too near existing housing, and therefore unacceptable (Home, 1982).

The withdrawal of the green belt relaxation (paragraph 32 of the appendix to circular 28/77 and circular 57/78) will materially reduce the options for Gypsies in counties which have substantial areas of green belt, making it even more important that development plans make specific criteria explicit. However, since development plans are not formally reviewed frequently, it will be many years before they all contain the detailed policies required by circular 1/94.

In another example, section 183 of the Planning and Compensation Act 1991 provides for 'stop' notices in relation to unauthorised caravan usage of land, but not against any other kind of unauthorised residential development, providing yet another weapon for use against travelling people.

For the Gypsy supporter it is not difficult to argue, in the face of these major difficulties, that the government's defence of the new approach to site provision (ie that it puts Gypsies on the same footing as any other private person seeking to provide a home and "they should seek planning consent like any other citizen") is somewhat less than realistic.

Definitions

Even before the 1968 Caravan Sites Act, the question of who qualified as a Gypsy was central to the political and social debate which we have traced in this volume. The Act itself attempted to settle the matter, but in practice has fuelled the argument ever since; an argument that has raged, not only in council chambers throughout the land, but in magistrate's courts, county courts and high court. In 1994 it ended in the appeal court.

The issue of definition is at the heart, not only of the process of site provision, but also of the race relations legislation and the draconian new law of criminal trespass. It is also at the centre of the process by which deeply embedded prejudice becomes structured into the laws which ostensibly seek to serve the minority groups most prone to discrimination.

If our Elizabethan forebears had problems with separating Gypsies from 'pretended egyptians', it is, in modern terms, the appearance of New Age Travellers which has brought the matter once more to a crisis. So much of the debate in the past has been confused by the notion of a mythical 'pure' or 'real' Gypsy who was seen to merit different and more favourable treatment than others; with the advent of New Agers, the argument is re-cast.

In commenting upon three legal cases, dealt with by way of judicial review in the high court (which were later subject to a hearing in the court of appeal), Beale and Geary (1994) point to a strong judicial desire to segregate the New Age Traveller from the Gypsy. In that case, Judge Harrison recognised that the definition of a Gypsy in the 1968 Act was "not a particularly happy one, although it may be that no better can be produced".

The case involved actions by three separate families of New Age Travellers, claiming to be Gypsies, against three local authorities: South Hams District Council, Gloucestershire County Council and Warwickshire County Council. The Travellers sought to quash the councils' decisions to evict them from land, and wanted orders of Mandamus, to provide them with adequate accommodation under the 1968 Act. The case was dismissed.

Under section 16 of the 1968 Act, Gypsies are defined as "persons of nomadic habit, whatever their race or origin ... but [this] does not include members of an organised group of travelling showmen, or persons engaged in travelling circuses, travelling together". But even before the introduction of this measure, Lord Chief Justice Parker had stated (in *Mills* v *Cooper,* 1967), "I think that 'Gypsy' means no more than a person leading a nomadic life with no fixed employment and no fixed abode. In saying that, I am hoping that these words will not be considered as the words of a statute, but merely as conveying the general colloquial idea of a Gypsy" (Beale and Geary, 1994).

In the same case, Lord Justice Diplock said: "I would define a Gypsy as a person with no fixed abode who leads a nomadic life, dwelling in tents or other shelters or in caravans, or other vehicles. If that meaning is adopted, it follows that being a Gypsy is not an unalterable status".

Thus it is recognised from the outset that, for the purposes of interpreting the 1968 Act, simply being a Gypsy would not be sufficient. It would be necessary to demonstrate a Gypsy way of life. Thus, in *Horsham District Council* v *Secretary of State* (1989), it was held that a Gypsy who had lost the nomadic habit of life did not remain a Gypsy for the purposes of the Act, even though he remained so by descent, culture, tradition or inclination.

Later judges added to the concept. Justice Leggatt in 1986 held that Gypsies were persons whom the Act contemplates "will live in caravans ... a type of person who, when he moves from place to place, does so with some purpose in view". This was refined by the House of Lords in *Greenwich LBC* v *Powell* (1988) when it was held that a person might be within the scope of the 1968 Act definition if they led a nomadic life only seasonally.

Subsequently, the courts began to address the issue of whether persons other than Gypsies might live such a Gypsy way of life. The fact that Travellers other than those traditionally recognised as Gypsies could fall within the definition was recognised by the DoE circular 28/77, which advised councils that the Act's definition "makes no distinction between different groups of Travellers or their trades, in law therefore, the term 'Gypsy' refers to a class of persons and is not confined to an ethnic group".

How then, with the court of appeal upholding the dismissal of the three new families' wish to be classed as Gypsies, does the law now stand? It was accepted by all parties to the action that the applicants were not Gypsies as traditionally understood, but came from conventional backgrounds before taking to travelling, spending time during the summer at festivals and doing casual agricultural work of a seasonal kind (Beale and Geary, 1994).

But whereas the applicants called themselves 'New Age Travellers' or 'hippies', their style of life was more or less "indistinguishable from that of traditional Gypsies", according to the vice-chair of the National Gypsy Council.   Judge Harrison, however, argued that more than this was required. The crucial test in his view is whether the applicant can indeed demonstrate "a nomadic habit of life". This requires more than just travelling or wandering. It requires "moving from place to place with a purpose in mind as a necessary and characteristic part of their lives". "Habit" said the judge, demands a "settled, enduring character of nomadic life not easily acquired" (Beale and Geary, 1994).

Beale and Geary argue that the judges, having now created, through a literal interpretation, a non-ethnic statutory definition which is capable of embracing people other than traditional Gypsies, have also devised a test so as to exclude such non-traditional groups. Given the minimal protection afforded by the 1968 Act in the courts, it is not much more than rhetorical tokenism to now exclude the New Age groups from even that level of protection.

It is important to note that the decision does not find that New Age groups are not Gypsies. Rather, in deciding who is covered by the 1968 Act, it is a matter for decision by the local authority in each case, on the basis of the available evidence, but the court has indicated that persons other than traditional Gypsies will need to provide strong evidence to establish the necessary purpose and enduring character of their nomadism. The word Gypsy, said the appeal court judge, means more than wandering from place to place "merely as the fancy takes them". Parliament, he said, had not intended to confer a special benefit on those who simply moved from place to place.

Deciding who is included

For the bemused officer of a local authority faced with making decisions as to who can be allocated a pitch and who is to be included in the counting process, the new judgement suggests that a range of questions need to be posed. If there has to be some recognisable connection between the wandering or travelling and the means of earning a livelihood, then for administrations and local government officers faced with implementing this definition in practice, at least ten questions arise:

1. whether there is a family history or tradition of travelling and related work patterns as a way of life;

2. whether there is evidence of an extended family network of Travellers;

3. whether the person follows a traditional Gypsy way of life and culture;

4. whether the decision to travel has been a result purely of homelessness or poverty, or to 'drop out' of settled society;

5. whether the travelling history of the applicant is of an enduring, long-term nature;

6. whether travelling has been for a particular purpose;

7. whether the purpose is economic in nature;

8. whether there is an intention to continue a travelling mode of life;

9. whether the person is an applicant for a pitch;

10. whether the family resorts to or resides in the area.

For one local authority at least, the high court case of 1994 has prompted an attempt at the encapsulation of the semantics into a definitive description, to be applied in all cases. In Warwickshire, it will be necessary to meet the following ordinance, to get a place on a site:

> For the purposes of the Caravan Sites Act 1968, a person is of nomadic habit of life, and therefore a Gypsy, if he has a settled and enduring way of life travelling from place to place for an identifiable, generally economic purpose. A person is not of nomadic habit of life if he is living in a caravan or vehicle simply because he has nowhere else to live, if his travelling is aimless, if he is travelling temporarily away from a permanent home, or if his travelling is short-lived, either recently adopted or not intended to continue in the long term.

> A person of such nomadic habit of life may be said to reside in or resort to the county if he has his usual abode here, or if, in his travelling way of life, he makes a practice of coming to the county to follow the purpose of travelling.

> A nomadic habit of life may be taken up or abandoned. It is neither necessary nor sufficient to belong to a Gypsy race or

to have been brought up as a child in a travelling family. But these facts may be relevant because the longer the habit of life has endured and the more deeply rooted it has been in an ethnic or family background, the longer a period settled in one place will be needed before the habit of life is to be regarded as lost, particularly where a travelling family occupies a residential site provided under the Act. Conversely, the necessary purpose and settled, enduring character of a nomadic habit of life are not easily or quickly acquired and after travelling for a relatively short period a person who stops travelling, or loses his purpose for doing so, may quickly be regarded as having lost his nomadic habit of life. (Warwickshire County Council, 1994)

Exclusions

What, then, of those who fall outside these definitions? In a county such as that which is the subject of our case studies, Avon, it means that large numbers will not meet the requirements. The case study demonstrated that considerable numbers of children who currently live on unofficial sites will face eviction. The education service and the primary health care which has intermittently been available may no longer be possible. This is not necessarily because those responsible withdraw, but rather because the cycle of stopping and moving from one unsatisfactory site to another will be increased and speeded up.

It is not at all clear that public policy has been advanced by the apparent resolution of the issue of definition. Essentially the debate about definition relates to who qualifies to get on sites provided under the 1968 Act. The same issue does not arise over questions of providing education, social welfare services and health care. In these services universal access is part of the law, and whether one is itinerant for any discernible purpose or not, makes no difference to one's right to the service. It is, however, easy to see that rejection or exclusion from the right to a pitch makes every difference to the possibility of being able to avail oneself of the other services. This is a contradiction or dysfunction of public policy which will, in due course, have to be faced. Indeed, for the policy analyst who would seek to predict the future, there are alternative scenarios - two possible endings.

As we have shown in Chapter 2, Gypsies had wandered across Europe and Asia for perhaps 500 years before they arrived in the British Isles. It is not unreasonable to suppose that those who came then and subsequently were not 'pure' Romany, but had inter-bred with the indigenous communities over time.

Contemporary references indicate that the attractions of the nomadic life soon brought others onto the open road. Oppressed peasants at the mercy of church and landlord may well, on occasion, have viewed the alternative way of living as at least as attractive as the one they had. The roads of Tudor England were, in any case, alive with vagrants, peddlers, hawkers and cony-catchers.

The perpetual journey of the Gypsies has always had attractions for others - one possible reason for the suppression they have always received from the state. And in each generation, 'pretended egyptians' have received even harsher treatment than supposed real ones.

What is enacted in the Criminal Justice and Public Order Act 1994 follows the same pattern of response to a newer wave of young people, who, for all the reasons discussed above, ranging from homelessness to a rejection of majority values, have taken to the road. Many of their children already know no other life. Some will eventually revert to the domestic, settled existence from which they sprang, others will merge, imperceptibly, into the generational pattern of the traditional travelling people, among whom they will find their only friends and sympathisers. Thus has it always been, and the finely-honed legal semantics of high court judges will cease to have meaning. The struggle to become 'legal' will continue.

The alternative scenario, and one which is implicit in the government's policy, is that the very continuation of the Gypsy lifestyle becomes not only less attractive, but harder to sustain.

Ministers have made it clear that Gypsies should be encouraged into housing; that in due course, and without undue pressure, they should see the advantages of a settled way of life. The education, health and social welfare services to which they would gain access, would mean a diminution of the urge to travel. In the words of the DoE consultation document: "It might be feasible to introduce a limited form of financial assistance towards the purchase of permanent housing for Gypsies who vacate pitches" (DoE, 1992). In this scenario, the problems of Gypsies and non-Gypsies, and sites and planning conditions, would disappear altogether.

The missing voice

The one vitally interested voice absent from much of this debate has been that of the Gypsy and travelling peoples themselves, whose muted and uncoordinated viewpoint underscores their lack of a coherent, unified political stance.   In researching an earlier generation of Gypsies and Travellers, Acton has distinguished four quite distinct sets of reactions, based upon combinations of values, by Gypsy people to the kind of debate within the settled society which this volume has traced.   His typology is summarised in Figure 7.

It is possible to discern elements of each of these reactions within the communities of Gypsies and Travellers of the 1990s, whether of the traditional kind or more recent recruits to the nomadic life. On the other hand, it is not at all clear that 25 years of legal, rent-paying and tax-paying existence on official sites has been a catalyst for cultural change within the terms of these definitions.

Indeed, the possibility of cultural disintegration, resulting from long-term settlement on council sites rather than because of economic collapse, cannot be discounted. There are clear signs of a creeping welfare dependency, of the kind described by right wing philosophers as endemic in the settled underclass. The universal access to television, now apparent on every Gypsy site, official and unofficial, is another element in the 'cultural adaptation' - and one which would repay future research in the ongoing debate about assimilation and absorption of the Gypsy way of life.

These diverse responses to the political and social tensions which Gypsy policy has provoked in the British context, do not encourage the hope that a coordinated and sustained voice will emerge in support of a rational alternative to the Criminal Justice and Public Order Act 1994. Is it reasonable, then, in the light of the detailed story traced in this volume, to characterise British policy as a form of 'ethnic cleansing'? What is usually meant by that term is the forced and wholesale removal of people, by reason of ethnicity, nationality or religion, from one place to another. In the Balkan civil war of the 1990s, where the phrase originally gained currency, ethnic cleansing formed part of the horrifying conflict between Serbs and Croats, Bosnians, Muslims and Christians in the factional fighting among the nations which made up the former Yugoslav Republic, and was pursued in civil war, murder and violence on a scale which civilised Europeans had not thought to see again.

Figure 7: **Cultural adaptation by Gypsies and Travellers, Acton's typology**

'Conservation'	Gypsies minimise their cultural contact with the outside world and either oppose or are apathetic to any change in their way of life.
Cultural disintegration	Gypsies become impoverished and demoralised, losing self-respect and self-confidence; collapse of their economy destroys the will to resist the dominant cultural perspectives of the host society.
Cultural adaptation	Gypsies accept influences from other cultures but as a bonus rather than replacement; nationalist tendencies among Gypsies are a form of cultural adaptation, seeking a new status within the host society.
'Passing'	Gypsies decide to compete with Gaujos on their own terms, concealing their origins; essentially, integration by individual decision.

Source: After Acton (1974, p 35)

But fundamentally, the experience of the Gypsies and Travellers of England and Wales, whose story we have been following through modern public policy responses, is no different. Instead of guns, it is the law which enforces the process.

Through mechanisms such as designation and the planning laws, through the failure of successive ministers to use the powers given them by parliament, and through pressures to be assimilated set out in the Criminal Justice and Public Order Act 1994, a people who claim a common ethnicity are legally unable to pursue their way of life in vast tracts of Great Britain. Many more people who share the lifestyle of the Gypsies are unable to stop in these areas without breaking the law.

Whether these issues are argued in terms of civil liberties or of the European Convention on Human Rights, or on the more difficult premises of societal prejudice and discrimination, it remains true that underlying British policy is an understated and somewhat ambiguous proposition that Gypsies should, in due course, become something other than nomadic; they should become house-dwelling, sedentary, settled people who are assimilated into conventional society, taking on all the values and characteristics, economic, financial, social and communal, which settled society embraces.

This, it could be argued, is a new form of ethnic cleansing not previously envisaged and the power of such a proposition is in the access which it offers to rights which are basic to citizenship: education, health care and social welfare. Such access is either impossible or, as our case studies have shown, at best precarious for Gypsies and Travellers who have no site to stop upon legally.

Thus society makes it more and more difficult to be nomadic by limiting the possibility of legal travel; it makes little effort to ensure access to the services of the welfare state by those who do travel. This form of ethnic cleansing bases itself on the proposition that any lifestyle which does not embrace permanent house-dwelling is best eradicated. It is as if snails - nature's other species that carry their homes with them - were made to leave their shells neatly, and in rows, under one leaf and come back to them each night!

To state the argument in such trenchant terms which, despite the evidence adduced in this volume, will seem to many extreme and exaggerated, is not to argue in favour of criminal trespass, unlicenced 'rave' concerts or the kind of irresponsible desecration which many unauthorised encampments present. Indeed, it is not our intention to argue in favour of anything that Gypsies may do which is offensive to their neighbours. The case for ceding full citizenship, civil rights, benefits and legality to Gypsies is the same case as for any other race or minority group with a legitimate right to be here. It is premised upon respect for difference, tolerance of non-conformity and regard for that essential dignity which resides in any group or community which holds to long-held values and tradition, in spite of any and every onslaught. It is to recognise that, in the end, such people add to, rather than jeopardise, the society we seek to uphold.

And yet it is possible, given the reinforcement of minority rights which the EU has begun to assert, to have a scintilla of optimism. We turn in the final chapter of this volume to a brief look at past and present attempts to articulate the Gypsy point of view and at the new European perspectives which may alter the so far minimal impact which they have had on the decisions made about them.

eight

THE GYPSY VOICE:
A EUROPEAN POSSIBILITY

The very notion of Gypsydom is antipathetic to the creation of a coherent programme of action or campaign for recognition and respect for Gypsies in the modern world. There is no Zionist dream to act as the central, unifying nexus like that which sustained the Jews throughout a 2,000 year diaspora. No religious faith or body of literature unites, through time and space, a Romany people; even the common language is a poor fragmented thing, long since degenerated to a crude patois, only of philological interest.

It has been argued that nomadism and the in-bred separateness which Gypsies and Travellers maintain against every challenge by modern society, every upheaval and revolution, makes it inevitable that attempts to give political voice to this minority group and its more recent adherents are doomed to failure.

Earlier attempts at creating an international movement have, for the most part, been led by non-Gypsy apologists such as Grattan Puxon and have made little impact on behalf of a people who want political and human rights without political and social assimilation. It is, so far, true that one is not possible without the other. Even to refer to Gypsies as a 'people' is problematic when, as Liegeois points out, there is no word in their vocabulary which designates them as a whole (Liegeois, 1986, p 57).

The formal sessions of the World Romani Congress of 1971 attempted to introduce a form of Zionist zeal which was immediately obscured in controversy over whether the idea of a 'nation state' was either wanted or appropriate. Instead, a somewhat romantic notion of 'Romanistan' was promulgated by leading spokesmen: rather more an emotive symbol of brotherhood, to be created 'in our hearts', than any aspiration to a nationhood with geographical meaning (Kenrick, 1971). Puxon's 'Rom nationalism' is, likewise, a fanciful call to militant action which never went beyond the dozen or so more plangent activists of the Gypsy Council.

As Acton points out, those espousing such ideas are likely to be literate, write books and use sophisticated methods to influence policy makers. "The illiterate nomad by the roadside is protected by his very isolation from the psychic oppression of a host society which considers him inferior" (Acton, 1974).

Groups in Spain, France and Finland have attempted, without apparent success in the last 25 years, to establish cross-national links between Gypsies. Bodies as diverse as the International Evangelical Gypsy Mission and the Communist Gypsy Organisation have espoused the concept of an international movement of Gypsies which would unite its adherents in a coordinated fight for civil rights and equal opportunities throughout the world.

Such attempts have, however, highlighted the size of the Gypsy population in Europe and the critical social problems now arising for nomadic groups. Political volatility flowing from the collapse of the Eastern bloc, the unification of Germany and the re-drawing of national boundaries in the emerging central European democracies, has resulted in large-scale migrations, some of them forced, with attendant racial strife.

But a different picture is emerging within the countries of the EU, and one which offers hope of a more constructive outcome. There are up to 1.8 million Gypsies and Travellers estimated to live within the twelve countries of the EU (see Table 13).

In July 1994 the first Gypsy Congress of the EU was held and was led by an MEP who is himself a Gypsy. It formulated a series of demands in the fields of social policy, civil liberties, literacy and the rights of women. But it is in the development of education for young Gypsies and Travellers that the EU has made most progress.

As we have seen in Chapter 3, EU policy regarding the education of Gypsy and Traveller children is set out in Resolution 89/C153/02 of 22 May 1989. This describes the plight of Gypsies and the context within which action is needed. It asserts that Gypsies' and Travellers' culture and language have formed a part of European heritage for over 500 years. With a Gypsy population of up to 1.8 million, it suggests that over half are children. The importance of encouraging school attendance and developing literacy is a prime objective.

Table 13: Numbers of Gypsies and Travellers in EU countries

	Minimum	Maximum
Belgium	10,000	15,000
Denmark	1,500	2,000
France	280,000	340,000
Germany	110,000	130,000
Greece	160,000	200,000
Ireland	22,000	28,000
Italy	90,000	110,000
Luxembourg	0,100	0,150
Netherlands	35,000	40,000
Portugal	40,000	50,000
Spain	650,000	800,000
UK	90,000	120,000

Source: Centre de Recherches Tsiganes

The Resolution is premised on the fact that only 30% to 40% of Gypsies within the EU attend school with any regularity, that over half have never been to school and that only a tiny percentage ever get into secondary education.

EU policy now asserts the importance of schooling within Gypsy communities, emphasises the changing environment, and promotes a set of measures aimed at improving access. These include, for example, the promotion of innovative teaching methods, the dissemination of lessons and the training of specialist teachers, especially those with a Gypsy origin.

Most importantly, a substantial part of the inter-cultural education budget is allocated to pursuing these aims; projects which promote international cooperation among educationalists are now a regular part of the EU programme. Language and history projects, production of teaching materials and the support of local initiatives are an integral part of the work. The Maastricht Treaty and the SOCRATES programme both highlight the importance of open and distance learning. A similar and more concentrated campaign has been running in parallel to that of the EU, organised by the Standing Conference of Local and Regional Authorities of the Council of Europe (SCLRAE). In a report dated 15 April 1993 (CPL(28)10) this body expressed concern that earlier initiatives had produced little response or positive action; indeed, it suggested "There is now an emergency" (SCLRAE, 1994).

SCLRAE's activities cover the whole of Europe, where, it states, there are between 6.5 and 8 million Gypsies. It proposes to set up new networks of municipalities most involved with Gypsy communities, to publish case studies of successful local initiatives, and to urge much greater participation and consultation with Gypsy people in the construction of policies which affect them.

It is not entirely clear, however, in the absence of a clear structure of representative bodies which can articulate the cohesive voice of the Gypsy peoples, how such consultative mechanisms are to work. It seems logical to localise these functions to the maximum degree possible, so that local initiatives are negotiated with local travelling communities. But this, in a sense, militates against any drive towards an international approach to major issues. Nevertheless, these activities represent a beginning, which, at least within the EU, could be a force for change and for the end of oppression.

It is, quite obviously, a small beginning and inevitably at risk of being obscured in the much wider effort to promote the rights of minority groups generally within the EU. The Council of Europe is preparing plans for a new framework convention on the protection of national minorities, linked to the European Convention on Human Rights. The Committee of Ministers signed this in November 1994. It is not without irony that they signed the Convention in the same week that the Criminal Justice and Public Order Act received Royal Assent. These initiatives can only bode well for the cause of Gypsies and Travellers. Given the depth of the discriminatory mechanisms even in one member state, which this volume has demonstrated, and the most recent, overtly prejudicial measures of the Criminal Justice and Public Order Act passed in the UK Parliament as recently as 1994, it is an international initiative which must be welcomed. Whether it is conducive to the growth of a European-wide voice for all the Gypsies and Travellers, New Age and other recent nomad groups, is yet to be seen.

REFERENCES

ACERT (1977) *Newsletter*, September.

ACERT/NATT (1986) *Post-Chester proposals*, Sawbridgeworth.

Acton, T. (1974) *Gypsy politics and social change*, London: Routledge.

Acton, T. (1991) 'Defining the limits of tolerance: UK government policy on Gypsies', *Roma* (Journal of the Indian Institute of Romany Studies), no 35.

Allison, G.T. (1971) *Essence of decision*, Boston: Little and Brown.

Allport, G.W. (1982) *The nature of prejudice*, 4th edn, Philippines: Addisson-Wesley.

Avon County Council (1975) 'Gypsy and Travellers subject plan', unpublished, planning department, ref: RWS/LCP, 24 June.

Avon County Council (1985a) Letter from director of education, dated 14 May.

Avon County Council (1985b) Minutes of an internal meeting in the education department, dated 15 November.

Beale, A. and Geary, R. (1994) 'New age Gypsies?', *Solicitors Journal*, 11 February.

Bell, L. and Malia, E. (1992) *Services for travelling people*, Birmingham: Centre for Community Health.

Borde, A. (1547) 'The first book of the introduction of knowledge', quoted in the *Journal of the Gypsy Lore Society*, New Series (1).

Boushel, M. (1994) 'The protective environment of children', *Journal of the British Association of Social Workers*, vol 24, no 2, pp 173-190.

Boynton, Sir J. (1986) 'Judicial review of administrative decisions: a background paper', *Public Administration*, vol 64, no 2.

Camm, E. (1934) 'Hurtwood School', *Journal of the Gypsy Lore Society*, vol XIII, no 4.

Clebert, J-P. (1963) *The Gypsies,* London: Vista.

Cornwell, J. (1984) *Improving health care for Travellers*, London: Kings Fund/Save the Children Fund.

Courtauld, S. (1994) 'Something nasty in the tealeaves', *The Spectator*, 8 January.

Cox, O.L. (1948) *Caste, class and race*, New York: Doubleday.

Crossman, R. (1977) *Diary of a cabinet minister*, vol 1, London: Cape.

Crout, L. (1987) *Traveller health care project: facilitating access to the NHS*, Walsall: Walsall Health Authority.

Dodds, N. (1966) *Gypsies, Didikois and other Travellers*, London: Johnson.

Durward, L. (ed.) (1990) *Traveller mothers and babies*, London: Maternity Alliance.

Feldman, D. (1988) 'Judicial review: a way of controlling government?', *Public Administration*, vol 66, no 1.

Fraser, A. (1993) *The Gypsies*, Oxford: Blackwell.

Gordon, P. (1992) 'The racialisation of statistics', in R. Skellington and P. Morris, *Race in Britain today*, London: Sage/Open University.

Hawes, D. (1987) 'Gypsy policy: a failure of both carrot and stick', *Policy and Politics*, vol 15, no 3.

Hawes, D. (1993) *Power on the back benches?*, Bristol: SAUS Publications, School for Advanced Urban Studies, University of Bristol.

Hawes, D. (1988) Recorded interview with DoE official.

Hawes, D. (1994) Informal interview with an Avon Traveller.

Hogwood, B. and Gunn, L. (1984) *Policy analysis and the real world*, Oxford: OUP.

Hogwood, B. (1987) *From crisis to complacency: shaping public policy in Britain*, Oxford: OUP.

Home, R. (1984) 'The Caravan Sites Act 1968: progress and problems with designation', *Journal of Planning Law*, April.

Home, R. (1987) 'Gypsies and the Caravan Sties Act: the designation numbers game', *Local Government Policymaking*, vol 14, no 3, pp 49-53.

Home, R. (1982) 'Planning problems of self-help Gypsy sites', *Journal of Planning and Environmental Law*, April.

Husband, P. (ed) (1982) *Race in Britain*, London: Hutchinson.

Hyman, M. (1989) *Sites for Travellers*, London: London Race and Housing Unit.

Judges, A.V. (1965) *The Elizabethan underworld*, new edn, London: Routledge.

Kenrick, D.S. (1971) 'The First World Romani Congress', *Journal of the Gypsy Lore Society*, series 3, no 4.

Liegeois, J-P. (1986) *Gypsies: an illustrated history*, London: Al Saqi.

Lindblom, C.E. (1959) 'The science of muddling through', *Public Administration Review*, no 19, pp 517-26.

Lloyd, L. (1993) 'Proposed reform of the 1968 Caravan Sites Act', *Critical Social Policy*, no 38, pp 77-84.

Mercer, P. (1992) *The education of Traveller children*, a report of a seminar organised by the Department of Education and Science in December 1991, London: DFE.

NGEC (1971) *The national Gypsy schools*, unpublished report by A. Ivetts.

O'Higgins, K. (1992) 'Travelling children in substitute care', a conference workshop paper given to a conference on 'Surviving Childhood Adversity' at Trinity College, Dublin, July.

Okely, J. (1983) *The travelling Gypsies*, Cambridge: CUP.

Pahl, J. and Vaile, M. (1988) 'Health and health care among Travellers', *Journal of Social Policy*, vol 17, pt 2.

Peck, B. (1983) 'Gypsies: a Sheffield experience', *Health Visitor*, no 56, p 583.

Reiss, C. (1975) *The education of travelling children*, London: The Schools Council.

Riding, M. (1985) 'The serological surveillance of immunity to various infectious agents', unpublished MSc dissertation, University of Glasgow.

Ridley, F.F. (1984) 'The citizen against authority', *Parliamentary Affairs*, vol 37, no 1, p 32.

Ruston, A. (1990) 'Family planning for Travellers', *Community Outlook*, November.

Save the Children Fund (1994) Counsel's Opinion by Peter Duffy, London, May, unpublished.

SCLRAE (1993) *Gypsies in Europe: the role of local and regional authorities*, by Gemesci and O'Brien (CPL(28)10) Strasbourg: Council of Europe.

Simon, H. (1958) *Administrative behaviour*, New York: Macmillan.

Smith, C. (1984) Informal interview with a Gypsy woman.

Smith, G. (1880) *Gypsy life*, London.

Smith, D., Gmelch, S. and Gmelch, G. (1982) *The special accommodation needs of Irish and other long distance Travellers*, Leicester: Leicester Polytechnic.

Solomos, J. (1989) *Race and racism in contemporary Britain*, Basingstoke: Macmillan.

UBHT (1993) Report of the specialist health visitor for travelling families, May 1990 to November 1992, unpublished, by Dolores Nelligan, Bristol: United Bristol Healthcare Trust.

University of Hertfordshire (1993) *The education of Gypsy and Traveller children*, Hatfield: ACERT.

Warwickshire County Council (1994) Policy document defining allocation practices for access to Gypsy sites in the county.

Government papers and official reports

1. Circulars and advisory notes

DoE circular 28/77 'Caravan Sites Act 1968 Part II', London: DoE

DoE circular 57/78 'Accommodation for Gypsies: summary of responses to the Cripps Report', London: DoE.

MHLG circular 49/68 (Welsh Office 42/68) 'Caravan Sites Act 1968', London: MHLG.

DoE (1969) Development Control Note no 8, 'Caravan Sites', London: DoE.

2. Hansard debates

Hansard (1908) The main debates on the Childrens Bill can be followed in the House of Commons (10 February, cols 1432-38 and 24 March, cols 1251-300) and the House of Lords (28 October, cols 209-39 and 12 November, cols 458-98).

Hansard (1961) House of Commons debate on private member's Bill, 1 December, cols 789-870.

Hansard (1985) House of Commons debate on the Environment Committee report, 5 July, cols 350-60.

Hansard (1986) House of Commons debate on the peace convoy, 3 June, col 773.

Hansard (1990) House of Commons debate on the Environment Committee report, 10 July, cols 257-60.

Hansard (1993a) House of Commons debate on private member's Bill, 5 February, cols 585-649.

Hansard (1993b) House of Commons adjournment debate, 26 July, cols 970-76.

Hansard (1994) The House of Lords debate at report stage on the Criminal Justice and Public Order Bill, 11 July, cols 1516-64.

3. Official reports and discussion documents

DES (1967) The Plowden Report: *Children and their primary schools*, London: HMSO.

DES (1983) *The education of Travellers' children,* HMI discussion paper, London: HMSO.

DFE (1994) *School attendance: policy and practice on categorisation of absence*, London: HMSO.

DES (1985) The Swann Report: *Education for all, the report of the Committee of Enquiry into the Education of Children from Ethnic Minority Groups*, London: HMSO.

DoE (1976a) Terms of reference for the Cripps Enquiry, dated February, London: DoE.

DoE (1976b) The Cripps Report: *Accommodation for Gypsies*, London: HMSO.

DoE (1982) *The management of local authority Gypsy sites*, June, London: DoE.

DoE (1985) 'Gypsy sites policy in England', memorandum, dated 12 December, London: DoE.

DoE (1986) *A report on the analysis of responses to consultation on the operation of the Caravan Sites Act 1968*, by G. Wibberley, London: DoE.

DoE (1987) *Gypsies and housing*, by Elizabeth Davies, London: DoE.

DoE (1991a) *Counting Gypsies*, by Hazel Green, OPCS, London: HMSO.

DoE (1991b) *Good practice guidelines for Gypsy site provision by local authorities*, by G. Todd and C. Clark, London: HMSO.

DoE (1991c) *Gypsy site provision and policy*, by G. Todd and C. Clark, London: HMSO.

DoE (1992) *Gypsy site policy and illegal camping*, consultation document, August, London: DoE.

HC 414 (1985) Third Report of the Environment Committee, Session 1984/5, London: HMSO.

MHLG (1967) *Gypsies and other Travellers*, London: HMSO.

INDEX

(References in italic indicate figures or tables)